Blister to Bliss

My Odyssey

Reframing Regrets...
moving from Guilt to Growth

Angela Odirin Afieghe

Copyright © 2024 Angela Odirin Afieghe
All Rights Reserved.

ISBN 978-1-915502-85-8

All intellectual property rights including copyright, design right and publishing rights rest with the author. No part of this publication may be copied, reproduced, stored, or transmitted in any way including any written, electronic, recording or photocopying without written permission of the author. This is a personal memoir, and the content is for your personal use and enjoyment only. It is not meant to replace any professional support you may need. The author does not assume liability for loss or damage caused by errors or omissions. Cover design by 2funkidesign. Published by Orla Kelly Publishing.

Dedication

This book is dedicated to my beloved children: Chisom, Cheryl Chidera, Chidozie Herbert, and Brandon Chiebunigom Onwukwe. Your unwavering support and enduring love have been the guiding light that illuminated my path through life's most challenging times. Thank you for being my constant source of strength and inspiration.

Acknowledgements

As I reflect on the journey that has led to the creation of "Blister to Bliss," I am overwhelmed with gratitude for the myriad of individuals whose support, wisdom, and encouragement have been instrumental in bringing this book to fruition.

First and foremost, I extend my heartfelt thanks to my family. Your unwavering love, patience, and belief in my vision have been my anchor and guiding light. I also want to thank my friend Wayne Purcell for his endless encouragement and my children for reminding me of the joy and wonder life holds, even in its most challenging moments.

I am deeply grateful to my mentor, Deirdre McLoughlin, whose insights and guidance have shaped this book, my personal and professional growth. Your wisdom has been a beacon during the most tumultuous storms.

To my publisher Orla Kelly, whose expertise and dedication have polished this manuscript into the gem it is today. Your tireless efforts and commitment to excellence have not gone unnoticed. I must also acknowledge the incredible team at Orla Kelly Publishing, whose enthusiasm and vision for this project matched my own from day one. Your support has been invaluable in bringing the 'Blister to Bliss' series to readers worldwide.

I want to thank my friends and colleagues at Nuvie Consulting for their constructive feedback and encouragement and the countless authors and thinkers whose work has influenced my own—thank you for lighting the path.

Finally, to you, the reader, for embarking on this journey with me. This book was written for you, hoping it will offer solace, inspiration, and a companion on your path to bliss.

This book is a fabric woven from the threads of many lives that crossed my path in my life journey. To all who have been a part of this journey, please know that you have my deepest gratitude and respect.

Thank you from the bottom of my heart.

Table of Contents

Acknowledgements v
Chapter 1: Introduction- The Blister Begins 1
    Lessons 8
    Exercises 13
Chapter 2: A Risky Departure 15
    Lessons 24
    Exercises 25
Chapter 3: The Friend Who Turned Foe 27
    Lessons 45
    Exercises 46
Chapter 4: Reframing Regrets 50
    Lessons 59
    Exercises 61
Chapter 5: Navigating the Blisters 68
    Lessons 74
    Exercise 76
Chapter 6: Rising from the Ashes 81

Lessons	89
Exercise	95
Chapter 7: The Path to Transformation	97
Lessons	104
Chapter 8: Blissful Beginnings	106
Lessons	113
Reflections	114
Afterword	122
About the Author	124
Please Review	125

About the Author

Born and raised in Delta state of Nigeria, Angela Afieghe is a performance-driven executive, holding the esteemed CEO position at Nuvie Consulting and spearheading EventBooth as its visionary founder.

She holds an MBA from University of Galway, Ireland, complemented by a foundational Electronics and Computer Engineering degree from Lagos State University, Nigeria. As of 2024, she studies Event Management at University College Dublin (UCD).

Endowed with industry-recognized credentials, Angela is a certified Project Management Professional (PMP) and Scrum Master, underpinned by her specialised education in project management from the University of Liverpool, UK, alongside a concurrent degree in IT Network and Infrastructure from Dublin Business School.

Angela's quest for knowledge extends to elite institutions worldwide, with immersive leadership and coaching programs at renowned institutions such as Harvard Business School and the distinguished Gabrielli School of Business at Fordham University in New York.

As a professional, Angela holds distinguished affiliations, including membership in the revered Project Management Institute,

MBA Association of Ireland, Network Ireland and Toastmasters International.

Angela's professional journey is enriched by an extensive tenure spanning diverse sectors such as Retail, Information Technology, Healthcare, Telecommunications, and Banking. This broad experience has fortified her expertise in multifaceted domains encompassing leadership, people management, business development, Information Technology, and Project Management, making her an invaluable asset in various industry landscapes.

In her enlightening book series Blister to Bliss, discover how Angela masterfully navigates the challenges of being a single parent while balancing her commitments to education and professional pursuits.

CHAPTER 1

Introduction- The Blister Begins

"The alchemy of life turns our wounds into wisdom and our blisters into bliss."

- Deepak Chopra (Simulated)

Who exactly am I? This question echoes across the pages of my life's Odyssey, bringing me from the depths of adversity to the pinnacle of triumph. My story is one of unrelenting tenacity, self-discovery, and the steadfast pursuit of happiness in hard times. It's a story that crosses borders and speaks to the global human spirit's ability to triumph despite hardship.

Originally from Oghara in Delta State, Nigeria, West Africa and now residing in Ireland, my life's Odyssey began at an astonishingly young age, laying the groundwork for a journey filled with obstacles, decisions, and profound transformations. At birth, I was given the name Angela, a name that carries with it hopes, resilience, desires, and the unbreakable energy of a mother. My father affectionately nicknamed me "Nuvie," a shortened form of Emuobomenuvie, signifying that what I possess surpasses the wealth of kings.

At 17, I met the man who would become my husband, kicking off ripples of events that would affect the rest of my life. By the age of 22, I had made the life-changing decision to marry, ushering me into adulthood and responsibility. I had no idea this union would be the first of many watershed occasions.

The decision to marry, often heralded as one of life's most significant choices, was, for me, a steep leap taken with a heart full of youthful rebellion rather than thoughtful consideration. At the tender age of 19, the world seemed ripe with possibilities. Yet, my understanding of those possibilities was naively narrow, driven by a desire to escape the confines of my parental home and embrace the freedom I believed adulthood promised. The choice to marry wasn't nurtured by love's deep, thoughtful roots but sprouted from a misguided quest for independence.

My partner, a man of 35, appeared as a figure of liberation. He was everything my constrained life was not: experienced, autonomous, and seemingly the gateway to the freedom I yearned for. He said the right things, and I believed him, and no one else could tell me anything different. The age difference, a gaping chasm of 16 years, was initially a badge of rebellion, a symbol that I was making my own choices, irrespective of societal norms or expectations. However, this disparity soon revealed itself as a fundamental barrier, not just in the trivialities of generational tastes but in the profound ways we communicated, dreamed, and viewed the world around us.

In my rush towards freedom, I bypassed the wisdom of those who had walked the path before me. Elders' advice, offered with the weight of experience, was dismissed as outdated and irrelevant to the modern love story I believed I was part of. This dismissal of guidance wasn't just a rejection of advice; it was a rejection of an opportunity to view my decisions through the lens of wisdom and foresight.

The aftermath of these decisions took time but unfurled gradually, like a slow tide pulling away to reveal the debris of haste and immaturity. Communication breakdowns became the norm, not because we didn't speak, but because the words we used were from different lexicons shaped by the eras we grew up in. The freedom I sought was there, but it was a hollow freedom encased within the confines of a relationship that was fundamentally misaligned from its inception.

With the burdens of a wife and a growing family on my shoulders, my life path took on new dimensions. The birth of my first child at 23 signified my entry into motherhood. This role would become crucial to my identity. As the years passed, I welcomed three more lovely children, each stretching my heart and challenging my spirit. The birth of my last child at the age of 35 added a poignant note to the symphony of my life, weaving together the threads of motherhood, profession, and self-discovery.

***

I grew up in a family with my parents and two older brothers. As my family's youngest and only girl, I was adored and pampered. My parents, both competent professionals, provided a solid foundation for my early years.

My father, an economist with a background in social sciences, worked tirelessly to achieve his academic goals. Scholarships allowed him to further his education at prestigious schools such as Loughborough University in England and other schools globally. His career path culminated in his position as Director of Cooperatives, Ministry of Commerce and Industry, Delta State, Nigeria. My mother, a kind nurse, was an essential community member, offering invaluable healthcare services. Her career progressed quickly, eventually culminating in her employment as the Deputy Director of Primary Healthcare at the Ministry of Health, Delta State, Nigeria.

I began my academic journey at four, starting with nursery school. I was in primary school by age six, avidly absorbing knowledge and life lessons. My journey continued when I began secondary school at eleven, eager to explore the ever-expanding study horizons. I started a new chapter in my academic and life adventure when I was sixteen, enrolling in a polytechnic in Enugu to study computer science. This was a massive change in experiences, which I will discuss later in this book. Later, I moved to Lagos to pursue an electronics and computer engineering degree.

This narrative transcends mere chronology, delving into the pivotal decisions, formidable challenges, and transformative experiences that have sculpted my odyssey. It presents an opportunity to impart the wisdom accrued and the resilience forged in the crucible of life and to celebrate the lessons distilled from a journey rich with trials and triumphs.

In offering these reflections, I aspire to create a beacon of inspiration and insight for you, the reader. I hope that within these pages, you will discover echoes of your unique journey, gaining perspectives illuminating your path and strategies to navigate the complexities of life. This book is a conduit for sharing the insights from my journey, accompanied by practical exercises and thoughtful reflections designed to guide you toward clarity and empowerment in confronting your challenges.

Through this shared exploration, may you find the tools to carve a path of growth and fulfilment, learning from the landscapes of my experiences to enrich your journey.

In my teenage years, I aspired to be a medical doctor. The presence of my mother, a dedicated medical professional, likely fuelled this desire. As the lone successor to her ambitions, I was expected to fill her shoes and eventually take over at St. Angela's Nursing Home and Maternity, which she had named after me. However, life, as it frequently does, took me on a different path. My adventure began at 17 when I enrolled in a polytechnic to study Computer Science; despite my mother's wishes for me to pursue medicine and stay closer to home, my father saw the promise in computer science and encouraged me to pursue it. So, I set forth.

My life in Enugu was a sharp contrast to my past experiences. I struggled with the intricacies of life because I was young and naive. I moved from a two-person room to a twelve-person dormitory, and the unfamiliar concept of hunger caught me off guard. I distinctly recall dialling my mother from a neighbouring Business Centre, complaining of problems with my stomach. She classified my condition as hunger after a quick interrogation, something I had unconsciously endured the entire day.

By my second year, I got acquainted with the school and made friends. Upon becoming independent for the first time, there were opportunities and obstacles, with peer pressure and influence playing a significant part. I quickly assimilated into numerous social groups and picked up a variety of habits, such as smoking and drinking. During this same time, I met the man who eventually became my husband and, later, my ex-husband.

In my first year of college in Enugu, a serendipitous encounter introduced me to a man named Herbert, an experience to remember! One day, as I strolled along, deep in thought, Herbert pulled up beside me in his car. Strikingly resembling Mary's (my friend and roommate) frequent visitor, I felt a sense of security in his presence. Despite some initial hesitation, I eventually agreed to join him on the short journey home, my memory failing me when it came to his name. Rather than ask, I opted not to risk hurting his feelings. However, instead of heading toward my house, Herbert detoured to a shoemaker's, insisting on crafting a pair of shoes for me, an offer I attempted to decline politely.

Subsequently, he suggested we dine out, citing an empty home as an incentive since my friends had yet to finish classes. Politely, I declined, expressing my contentment with returning home. Upon reaching my destination, Herbert dropped me off, and I offered thanks.

Later that evening, around six o'clock, Herbert returned bearing a considerable load of groceries and presents. Sensing my reluctance to meet him, my roommate informed him I was resting. Undeterred, he left the gifts behind. Herbert visited every other day for nearly two weeks, laden with various offerings. Fearful and unwilling to confront the situation, I refrained from seeing him.

Eventually, I confided in Mary about the persistent advances from her perceived boyfriend, only to discover she did not know of him, and he was not who I had assumed. They just shared the same car model and colour!

When Herbert reappeared, I decided to meet him, and after clarifying the misunderstanding, we laughed. His interest in pursuing a romantic relationship emerged. Still, I firmly declined due to my preconceived notions about his stature and attractiveness, exacerbated by my friend's ironic nickname, "Stoneface", bestowed upon him.

Unexpectedly, Herbert's demeanour shifted abruptly, demanding repayment for all the gifts he had bestowed upon me. Fearing him, I attempted to avoid him and temporarily left my home. However, he located me at the hostel where I was staying with a friend, forcefully held my hand, and presented a menacing request— that I either enter into a relationship or repay all the money he spent on me. Panic-stricken, I cried out for help, drawing the attention of fellow students who intervened. So, one of the students named Mark asked him to leave me alone. Herbert turned around angrily and gave him a slap across his face, and a fight ensued between the two men. In a desperate move, Herbert released tear gas to disperse the onlookers.

This attracted the attention of the campus police, and both men were apprehended, which led to us being summoned before a disciplinary panel. Our academic futures hung precariously in the balance, and my mind raced with dread at the prospect of my parent's reaction. The looming question of what I could tell them gnawed at me.

Through desperate pleas and appeals, we received a brief suspension, allowing us to continue our studies. This harrowing incident left an indelible lesson etched in my psyche: never accept gifts from individuals without scrutinising their intentions. My instinctual response to such offers became a resolute inquiry: "What is expected in return?"

Upon graduation, I embarked on a journey to Lagos to secure direct entry into Electronics and Computer Engineering. This pivotal shift required relocating to Lagos, Nigeria.

Lessons for my 17 years old self

Navigating relationships and understanding the implications of accepting gifts from others, especially from men, can be complex.

- Understand the Intentions: Try to discern the intentions behind a gift. Gifts can be a genuine expression of affection or friendship, but they can sometimes carry expectations. It's important to consider why someone is giving you a gift and what it might imply about your relationship with them.
- Maintain Independence: Accepting gifts, costly ones, can sometimes create a sense of obligation. Remember that you are never obligated to reciprocate feelings or favours just because someone gives you something. Your autonomy and ability to make free choices should always be preserved.
- Set Your Boundaries: It's okay to set boundaries about what gifts you are comfortable accepting. If a gift makes you uncomfortable or implies more than you are willing to give in return, it's perfectly acceptable to decline politely.
- Communicate Clearly: If you accept or decline a gift, communicate your decision. If accepting, express gratitude. If declining, do so kindly and honestly, explaining that while you appreciate the gesture, you don't feel comfortable accepting the gift.
- Value Relationships over Material Things: Focus on building relationships based on mutual respect, shared interests, and genuine affection rather than on material exchanges. A gift can never substitute for the foundational elements of a healthy relationship.
- Trust Your Instincts: Always trust your instincts. If something doesn't feel right about the way someone is giving you gifts,

listen to that feeling. Your intuition is a powerful tool for guiding you toward healthy relationships and away from potentially harmful situations.

Navigating interactions with others, especially regarding gifts, is part of growing up. Remember, every decision you make is an opportunity to learn more about your values, boundaries, and relationships you want to cultivate.

General Lessons

- The Importance of Self-Knowledge: Understanding one's needs, desires, and motivations is crucial before making life-altering decisions. My first misstep was marrying to escape a situation and meet other people's expectations rather than to embrace a partnership, highlighting the need for introspection and self-awareness.

- Age is More Than Just a Number: While age-gap relationships can be successful, they require a deep understanding and respect for the differences that come with disparate life stages in my case. Communication barriers and differing life perspectives underscored how significant those gaps can become.

- Value of Guidance: Disregarding the advice of those with more experience was a manifestation of youthful arrogance. Though elders' wisdom may not always align perfectly with one's desires, it is a valuable compass that can help navigate complex decisions.

- Understanding Love and Freedom: True freedom in adulthood is not about escaping constraints but making choices that align with your core values and long-term happiness. Love and partnership should enhance that freedom, not serve as a vehicle for its pursuit.

Reflecting on these lessons, the echo of my initial mistake serves not as a refrain of regret but as a clarion call for growth, understanding, and eventual healing. The journey through and beyond this mistake is a testament to the resilience of the human spirit and the capacity for change.

As you turn these pages, you may find yourself standing at the crossroads of heartache and healing, where the echoes of your past and the whispers of your future collide. The end of a relationship, whether through divorce, the loss of a partner, or the dawning realisation that you are trapped in a detrimental bond, brings with it an avalanche of emotions—a blend of sorrow, betrayal, confusion, and sometimes, relief. This chapter seeks to walk you through this turbulent storm, offering a guiding light as you navigate the initial shock and emotional turmoil that has upended your world.

The moment of loss can be compared to being plunged into icy waters, where the cold seeps into every pore, shocking your system into numbness. It is a sensation of disbelief, a fog that clouds your reality, making the familiar seem suddenly alien. This shock is your mind's way of protecting itself, a buffer against the rawness of your pain. It's okay to feel disoriented, to question the solidity of the ground beneath your feet. This feeling is a natural response to an unnatural rupture in your life's fabric.

Beneath the numbness, a storm brews—a tempest of emotions that can feel overwhelming in their intensity. Anger may surge, directed at your partner, yourself, or the world for its perceived unfairness. Sadness may wash over you in waves, deep, aching sorrow that hollows you out from within. Fear, too, makes its presence known, whispering uncertainties about the future and doubts about your worthiness of love and happiness.

Guilt may weave through these emotions if you regret how things ended or wonder about the paths not taken. A heavy chain can bind you to the past if not addressed.

Allow yourself to inhabit and acknowledge these feelings without judgment to move forward. This is not a sign of weakness but of profound strength. It requires courage to face your pain, sit with it, and understand its origins and impact on your heart and soul.

Understanding your pain means recognising that it is a part of you, but it does not define you. It is a chapter in your story, only part of the book. This pain can teach you to shape you into someone more resilient, empathetic, and more in tune with your own needs and desires.

Your journey through this pain is uniquely yours. While the path may be fraught with obstacles, it is also lined with opportunities for growth and self-discovery. In the coming pages, we will explore strategies for navigating this journey and transforming your pain into a foundation upon which you can build a future filled with hope, strength, and bliss.

Remember, you are not alone in this journey. Just as stars pierce the night sky, your darkest moments are illuminated by the light of your inner resilience. Step by step, breath by breath, you will traverse this terrain. From blister to bliss, your journey unfolds, and it starts with understanding your pain, embracing it, and ultimately, transforming it.

In the aftermath of a seismic shift in our worlds—be it the end of a marriage, the loss of a beloved partner, or the realisation of entrapment in a relationship that diminishes our spirit—the spectrum of emotions we encounter can be both bewildering and overwhelming. This section is an affirmation, a gentle but firm reminder of the power and necessity of acknowledging and accepting your feelings as they are. It is through this validation that the first steps towards healing are taken.

In the wake of such profound loss or realisation, your emotions may span the breadth of human experience. You might find moments of anger interspersed with pangs of regret or deep wells of sadness, suddenly giving way to brief sparks of relief or even unexpected joy at newfound freedom. This emotional kaleidoscope, though disorienting, is a natural response to the upheaval you've faced.

It's crucial to understand that there is no "right" or "wrong" way to feel. Society often imposes timelines and expectations on grief and recovery, suggesting a linear progression from sadness to acceptance. However, the reality of emotional healing is far from linear—it's a journey that zigs and zags, ebbs and flows, with everyone's path as unique as their fingerprint.

Validating your emotions does not mean resignation. Instead, it's about permitting yourself to feel whatever you feel without judgment or censorship. It's acknowledging that your feelings are real, valid, and meaningful. They are indicators of your profound capacity for love, commitment, and connection, even in the face of loss or betrayal.

By validating your emotions, you're taking a critical step towards self-compassion. This self-kindness is akin to applying a salve to a wound; it doesn't immediately heal the cut but soothes the pain and creates conditions conducive to healing.

Exercises

1. Journaling: Writing can be a powerful tool for emotional validation. It allows you to articulate your feelings, name them, and, in doing so, acknowledge their existence and their impact on you. There's no need for censorship or editing—let your thoughts and emotions flow freely.

2. Mindfulness and Meditation: Mindfulness practices can help you become an observer of your emotions, noticing them without becoming engulfed by them. Meditation, even for a few minutes daily, can allow you to breathe through your feelings and recognise and accept them as they come.

3. Seeking Support: Sharing your journey with family members, professionals such as therapists, and trusted friends can also serve as a form of validation. Speaking your truth out loud and having it acknowledged and accepted by others can reinforce the validity of your experiences and emotions.

4. Self-Affirmations: Simple affirmations tailored to reinforce self-validation can be powerful. Phrases like "My feelings are valid," "It's okay not to be okay," and "I give myself permission to feel" can serve as reminders of one's right to one's emotions.

You're laying the groundwork for genuine healing as you validate your emotions. This doesn't mean the pain disappears overnight; instead, you're building a foundation of self-respect and understanding from which you can begin to rebuild. Once acknowledged and accepted, your emotions become less like chains holding you back and more like signposts guiding you towards deeper self-understanding and eventual peace.

Remember, your journey through pain and into healing is not just about reaching a destination of "being okay." It's about growing in emotional integrity, learning to navigate the complexities of your feelings with grace, and emerging on the other side not just intact but empowered. Your emotions, in all their messy, beautiful complexity, are a testament to your humanity and your capacity for resilience. Validate them, and in doing so, validate yourself.

The obstacles I faced seemed big as I stood on the verge of departure. I was not travelling alone; instead, I was entrusted with caring for three small children and being pregnant with my fourth child. The logistics of leaving my country were intimidating, and the uncertainties ahead cast a shadow of doubt over my path.

I struggled with the significant hopes and doubts that followed my decision to relocate. It was a gamble, a plunge into the unknown motivated by the hope that physical isolation would be the key to mending a shattered relationship. The delicate dance between love, responsibility, and personal growth played out against cultural expectations and societal norms.

Actions

Separating Actions from Self-Worth - *The Two-Column List*

Create two columns on a piece of paper. In the first column, write down the actions or decisions you feel guilty or ashamed about. In the second, list the qualities and values that define you as a person. This exercise helps to separate your actions from your inherent worth, reminding you that mistakes do not determine your character.

CHAPTER 2

A Risky Departure

"Our greatest glory is not in never falling, but in rising every time we fall and finding the bliss that awaits."

- Confucius (Inspired)

Decisions can be complicated, especially when entwined with familial expectations, societal conventions, and personal desires. I was at the intersection of these complex influences. It was a period when the delicate balance between family commitments and the compelling need for distance hung in the balance, and my decisions weighed not only my future but the futures of my children and the expectations of people who loved me dearly.

In every story of transformation, pivotal moments serve as catalysts for change. These incidents shake us to our core, compelling us to confront the uncomfortable truths about our lives and the relationships we navigate within them. Such was the case on a seemingly ordinary Friday afternoon, unfolding into events illuminating a partnership's and household's complex dynamics. This narrative sheds light on the immediate shock and confusion experienced. It serves as a profound example of the underlying patterns and dynamics that can lead to feelings of entrapment or the dissolution of a relationship.

The incident, one of my wake-up calls, occurred after a routine couples' argument initially seemed mundane. It was a day filled with the usual responsibilities: overseeing businesses, preparing meals, and dedicating time to studies for a master's degree. However, a simple yet profound interaction about two slices of bread disrupted the day's normalcy. The refusal by a household staff member to provide food, under instructions that underscored a deeper issue of control and disrespect, became the catalyst for a moment of acute clarity.

Following an all-too-familiar spat with my husband on this luminous Friday afternoon, I absorbed the rhythm of my daily tasks. I ventured out to check on my businesses, a routine sweep to ensure everything ran smoothly. Later, I returned to the warmth of my home, where I busied myself with preparing dinner and cherishing moments with my children. The cycle of life seemed unremarkable yet comforting in its predictability.

The next day's dawn saw me rising at the customary hour of 6:30 am, diving headfirst into the academic demands awaiting me. I was deeply engrossed in pursuing a master's degree in project management from the prestigious University of Liverpool, and the morning hours slipped unnoticed as I dedicated myself to an assignment due by midnight. Only when a friend intervened did I realise the day had advanced and I had forgotten breakfast.

I asked my friend to request a simple meal from the housekeeper—just a few slices of bread and beans I had prepared the evening before. However, the response relayed back to me was nothing short of bewildering. The housekeeper, employed by me, had audaciously declared that the remaining bread was reserved for "Uncle's" breakfast the following morning and would not give me any.

Confusion and disbelief swirled within me as I processed her words. It was nearing 4 pm; my stomach was empty, and my employee challenged my right to food from my kitchen. Incensed and incredulous, I summoned her for an explanation. Meeting my gaze unflinchingly, she reiterated her stance, adding a layer of astonishment by revealing that my husband had specifically instructed her to manage the household's provisions in this manner, including a directive to exclude any purchases from any of my shops.

The revelation left me paralysed, a melange of shock and anger coursing through me. This wasn't just about bread; it was a stark manifestation of disrespect within the walls of my home, where I believed autonomy and respect were mutual. Trivial in its origin but profound in it's implications as it forced me to confront the unsettling dynamics of power and control that had silently infiltrated my life.

At its core, this incident reveals a power struggle that extends beyond the immediate disagreement. It highlights a dynamic where financial contributions and household responsibilities are wielded as tools of control and authority. The staff member's allegiance to one partner, influenced by financial provisions and explicit instructions, depicts an environment where respect and autonomy are compromised. This action questions the equitable partnership within the household and reflects broader issues of power, respect, and independence.

The dynamics of control in this scenario are multifaceted, involving not only the relationship between partners but also the relationships with those within the household. Restricting access to resources within one's own home, especially under the guise of financial management, reveals a pattern of overt and covert control. It challenges the notion of partnership and shared authority, placing one in a position where one's autonomy and dignity within one's home are undermined.

Such dynamics, particularly when they recur or are part of a broader pattern of behaviour, can lead to feeling trapped. Realising that one's autonomy is compromised, even in seemingly trivial matters, can illuminate the extent to which control permeates the relationship. In these moments of clarity, the feelings of entrapment crystallise physically, emotionally, and psychologically. The sense of being trapped stems not only from the actions of others but also from the realisation of how deeply these dynamics have taken root within one's own life.

This story serves as a poignant reflection on the complex interplay of dynamics within relationships that can lead to feelings of entrapment or the eventual end of a partnership. It prompts a deeper examination of how power, control, and respect manifest in our closest relationships and how these dynamics impact our sense of autonomy and worth. Understanding these dynamics is critical to the process of steering them. Regardless of whether you are addressing and renegotiating these patterns or deciding to step away from them. In acknowledging and analysing these dynamics, we take a crucial step toward reclaiming our autonomy and reshaping our relationships into partnerships of mutual respect and equality.

As I reflect on the turbulent period of my life before I left Nigeria, I am painfully aware of the weight of family expectations and cultural customs that hung over my head like a thundercloud. My parents, firmly rooted in their faith and community, held positions of power and respect in the church and the state. We were a family who took our catholic faith seriously, and the mere wish for isolation from my marriage could easily be misunderstood as a desire for divorce.

It was a problem that weighed heavily on my mind. On the one hand, I was yearning for emotional and physical distance to fix the cracks in my marriage. On the other hand, I was acutely aware that the distance could lead to further cracks, possible embarrassment, and disappointment in my decision, which could affect my parents and our close-knit community.

In managing this delicate balance, I knew that my family's love and support were pillars of strength in my life, and I treasured our close relationships. It was awful to think about causing them sorrow or disappointment.

But there was another fact I couldn't deny: the importance of self-preservation and recovery. The distance I sought was not a rejection of family values or faith but a search for personal growth and emotional healing. This internal conflict echoed within me daily as I remained in that position, divided between family expectations and my need for distance.

In these moments of doubt, I knew deep down that if I could survive this storm, I wouldn't be the same person who walked through it. I was about to embark on a journey that would undoubtedly transform me, but I was still wondering if my family would welcome the change or perceive it as a break from the principles we valued.

Ultimately, my decision to seek space was an act of self-preservation and a leap of faith towards healing, not a rejection of my family or our deeply held beliefs. It was a risk I was ready to take, even if it meant defying the expectations placed on me. The practical challenges of leaving Nigeria with three children and a pregnancy awaited me in the next phase of my journey. Still, the emotional fight had already begun, waged silently within the boundaries of my heart.

In the labyrinth of human relationships, societal expectations often serve as the invisible walls that confine us to paths not of our choice. These norms and standards, woven into the fabric of our culture, profoundly influence our personal lives, shaping our decisions and perceptions of happiness and success. Societal pressures compel us to remain in unhappy relationships or harbour guilt over their dissolution. By understanding these forces, we can dismantle the barriers they create, allowing ourselves the freedom to pursue genuine joy and fulfilment.

Most times, societal expectations— dictate the course of our relationships and our emotional responses to them. The belief that one 'should' stay in a marriage for the sake of appearances or that one 'must' sacrifice personal happiness for the perceived stability of the family exemplifies the heavy yoke of these norms.

As my marriage came to an end, I confronted a stark realisation: the dissolution of my relationship elicited little external reaction. The seismic impact I had anticipated —a narrative ingrained by societal and familial expectations—failed to materialise.

When a relationship ends, the departure from societal norms can often lead to an intense feeling of guilt. This guilt is not merely about the relationship but stems from a perceived failure to adhere to societal expectations. Most African girls are taught to view the end of a relationship as a personal failure rather than a step toward self-discovery and happiness. This perspective is a testament to the power of societal expectations in shaping our internal narratives, transforming the natural conclusion of a relationship into a source of shame and regret.

Another significant aspect of societal pressure is the fear of judgment from others. This fear can act as a chain, binding individuals to unhappy or unhealthy relationships. The anticipation of gossip, pity, or condemnation can be paralysing, leading many to endure misery rather than face social censure. It is a stark reminder of the role of external perceptions in our most intimate life decisions.

The journey to break free from societal expectations and constraints begins with recognising and accepting one's desires and needs as valid and vital. It involves rewriting the script of one's life to prioritise personal happiness and well-being over the approval of others. This process is not without its challenges, but it is a necessary step toward authentic living and loving.

Societal expectations, with their rigid definitions of success, happiness, and normalcy, influence our relationships. They can trap us in cycles of unhappiness and guilt, preventing us from pursuing paths that lead to genuine fulfilment. By recognising and challenging these pressures, we can reclaim our right to make choices that resonate with our deepest selves, paving the way for a life defined not by societal norms but by personal joy and satisfaction.

The decision to leave Nigeria was filled with emotional pain and logistical obstacles. As I stood on the verge of embarking on this life-changing Odyssey, I was acutely aware of the practical hurdles that lay ahead, especially given that I was carrying not only the weight of my past but also the weight of my future—a pregnancy.

In those moments of doubt, it felt as if the universe was conspiring to put my will and determination to the test. The notion of leaving seemed daunting, but I knew it was a necessary step.

The financial implication of that decision was that in addition to what was available, I had to sell my business and liquidate assets. I was willing to give up everything for a better future.

The practical parts of moving were intimidating. There were several issues to address, from obtaining travel documents for my children to planning for prenatal care during the pregnancy. This journey was a daring adventure for me.

Leaving behind the familiarity of my surroundings and the comforts of home was both freeing and terrifying. It was like going into the unknown. The dream of a better life for myself and my children beckoned, but the road ahead was difficult.

Everything seemed to be happening at once for me—a dysfunctional marriage, a relocation, and the anticipated arrival of a new life.

Despite these difficulties, I was tackling my concerns front-on, propelled by the possibility of success. I carried an unbreakable mindset of optimism, determination, and the unyielding belief that this challenging chapter of my life would lead to a more fantastic, rewarding future within me.

In the face of these difficulties, I knew I was making the right choice for myself and my children. With all its uncertainties and complications, this voyage demonstrated the enduring resilience of humans and the power of a mother's love.

The decision to leave Nigeria stemmed from a deep-seated yearning for change, a desperation that couldn't be ignored. My husband proposed that I move to the United States to live with his sister during my pregnancy, a plan that didn't align with my desires. Having previously experienced the warmth and hospitality of Ireland, my preference leaned strongly towards relocating there. Amidst a marriage fraying at the edges—riddled with unspoken grievances, unresolved conflicts, and unfulfilled expectations—the prospect of moving in with an in-law appeared less like a solution and more like a temporary palliative, failing to address the underlying issues we faced.

The emotional vacuum between my spouse and I appeared impossible, like an impassable gorge. However, I held to the hope that distance would provide the essential breathing space for healing and transformation.

However, when I began this life-changing journey, I couldn't shake the recurring uncertainties that clouded my optimism. The notion of patching up a broken relationship from thousands of miles away seemed intimidating. I wondered if physical distance could heal the emotional abyss that had grown over time. In those moments of doubt, I wondered if our relationship could withstand this ultimate test of distance and separation. I clung to the hope that physical isolation would give me emotional clarity as I settled into my new life in Ireland. The space between us may be a blank canvas on which we could create a new chapter in our story. I was willing to put my life on the line to re-establish a connection that had once brought me joy and camaraderie. The nagging worries were countered by the optimism that this journey might be a catalyst for transformation.

The darkest times in life can lead to new beginnings and better days. I clung to the dream that our relationship would rise from the shadows and find a fresh start. Despite my reservations, I trusted in the potential of transformation. The road ahead was unpredictable but also full of hope for healing and rediscovery. I knew that healing a damaged relationship would require patience, faith, and unrelenting perseverance as I faced the challenges from afar. I was about to embark on a voyage to an unknown destination but was joined. My companions were love, hope, the tenacious human spirit, and the Holy Spirit, who guided me through the hopes and fears ahead.

Lessons

- Conflict as Catalyst for Change: Angela's experiences illustrate how personal conflicts can catalyse profound personal and professional transformation, emphasising the importance of facing challenges head-on.
- Autonomy in Decision-Making: This narrative underscores the significance of maintaining autonomy in decision-making processes, particularly in environments where external control and power dynamics are prevalent.
- Navigating Family and Societal Expectations: The complexities of balancing personal desires against the weight of familial and societal expectations are a common challenge in professional environments where cultural norms influence career paths.
- Importance of Support Networks: The reliance on friends and one's broader support network during critical moments reflects the importance of cultivating robust support systems in achieving professional and personal goals.
- Strategic Risk-Taking: The decision to relocate and the associated risks underline the importance of strategic risk-taking to achieve substantial personal and professional growth.
- Recognising Unhealthy Dynamics: Recognizing unhealthy dynamics in any relationship, including professional ones, is crucial for maintaining a healthy work environment and personal well-being.
- Value of Independence: This narrative strongly emphasises the value of financial and emotional independence, which is also applicable in professional settings where independence can lead to innovation and leadership.

- The Transformative Power of being Focussed: Pursuing a master's degree amidst the challenges, illustrates the power of being focussed on your goals and personal development, reinforcing that education is a powerful tool for change.

Exercises

Here are some exercises to help you rediscover your value beyond your roles as a partner, mother, father, or caretaker.

Reflection: Beyond the Mirror

Consider how you measure your worth. Is it through the eyes of others, the roles you play, or the achievements you've accumulated? Reflect on the idea that your worth is intrinsic, not contingent on external validation or accomplishments. You are worthy simply because you exist.

Rediscovering your value beyond your roles as a partner or mother is a journey of self-discovery and affirmation. It's about seeing yourself through a lens of compassion and appreciation, recognising the depth of your worth, and embracing the unique qualities that make you unmistakably you. As you engage in these exercises and reflections, remember that this journey is not a destination but a continuous process of growth and self-love.

Mapping Your Life's Highs and Lows

1. Draw a line on paper to represent your life's journey. This could be horizontal or vertical.
2. Mark significant highs and low events along this line.

3. Reflect on these moments, focusing on what you learned about yourself through each experience. How did you grow? What strengths did you discover?

This exercise isn't about dwelling on the past but about recognising how your experiences have shaped the resilient and multifaceted person you are today.

4. Name all the roles you identify with (e.g., partner, mother, father, friend, career woman). Next to each role, list the qualities you bring to it. You might be surprised to see how much overlap there is, indicating core attributes that define you beyond any single role. This reflection reminds you that you are not defined by these roles but by the qualities you embody.

5. Set aside time to reflect on what makes you unique. Ask yourself, "What are three qualities I love about myself?" These can be characteristics, talents, or even quirks that make you, you. Write these down and remind yourself of them daily. Embracing your uniqueness is a step toward valuing yourself beyond societal or relational expectations.

Reflection: The Joy of Being You

Think about moments when you felt alive and true to yourself—moments when you were not fulfilling a role but simply being. What were you doing? Who were you with? Reflecting on these moments can guide you toward activities and relationships that align with your true self.

CHAPTER 3

The Friend Who Turned Foe

"Each betrayal begins with trust"

- Martin Luther.

As I stepped upon Irish soil, a sense of uncertainty swept over me. My journey had begun with the intention of mending a broken relationship. Still, it had also thrust me into a world of seclusion and unfamiliarity.

One of the most challenging issues I faced upon arrival in Ireland was an overpowering sensation of loneliness. The bustling streets of my city, the familiar faces of family and friends, and the reassuring rhythms of daily life were all gone. In their place was a peaceful, sometimes isolated, new reality.

The lack of a support network weighed heavily on me. I couldn't turn to my mum, siblings, or the close-knit group I had known for comfort and direction. I was in an unfamiliar geographical and mental terrain, and the road ahead was intimidating.

There was a terrible sense of loneliness that went far beyond the lack of company. It was a sensation of being adrift in a sea of unknown faces, country, and habits. Loneliness may be a relentless companion, especially when you are away from the warmth of family and friends, as I was. I realised loneliness was a chance to confront my inner self, battle with the solitary, and emerge more robust because of the experience.

However, it wasn't just the emotional isolation that was difficult; it was also the lack of a familiar support system. My family and friends had been my pillars of strength in Nigeria. They were the ones I went to when I needed help, the ones who provided a safety net through life's unavoidable falls. Now that I was far away in Ireland, I needed that safety net. The physical and emotional distance between me and my loved ones was palpable, frequently making me feel vulnerable. During these times, I realised the deep need for social support. While I was physically far from my family and friends, their love and support were unwavering. Regular phone calls, video chats, and messages served as an essential link between us over the miles.

My dearest friend, Mary, was a continuous source of comfort and encouragement. At the same time, I navigated the problematic pregnancy journey; she seized any opportunity to travel to Ireland from Nigeria to support me in every way she could. Taking care of domestic duties and making healthy meals weren't anything she hesitated to take on. The depth of our connection and the remarkable character and strength she possessed was demonstrated by her deeds of compassion and her sincere concern for my welfare. Mary's presence was a source of solace and a reminder of the value of true friendship in those times when I needed it most.

Social relationships are essential for our well-being. Loneliness and the absence of a support system can cause increased tension, anxiety, and physical health problems, harming our mental and emotional well-being.

While loneliness and the lack of a support structure were unquestionably tricky, they were also transforming. They pushed me to reach out, make contacts, and create a new support network in Ireland. Loneliness became a teacher, revealing my inner strength. At the same time, the lack of a support structure taught me the value of reaching out and building ties with people.

I overcame this problem by seeking opportunities to connect with others, which was challenging. I volunteered in charity organisations, joined local sports clubs, and participated in the local community church. Today, however, I have joined local and international community groups and attended various cultural events and social gatherings. But, amid the loneliness, moments of connection and unexpected friendships emerged. While initially intimidating, these exchanges gradually became a lifeline—a method to battle loneliness and build new connections.

I also learned the value of seeking help from the expat community. Many of the people I met were also traversing the maze of adaptation and understood my issues. Sharing stories, offering advice, and lending a sympathetic ear which fostered a sense of community that alleviated loneliness.

In her book "The Gifts of Imperfection," Brené Brown emphasises the significance of vulnerability in developing lasting connections. It was a lesson I learned during this time. I experienced a sense of relief and was able to connect with others on a deeper level after opening up about my emotions of loneliness and the lack of a support system. This served as a reminder that vulnerability, far from being a sign of weakness, can open the door to genuine human connection and be a therapy.

The struggles with loneliness were not without their lessons. In the silence of my new surroundings, I discovered an excellent chance for self-reflection and self-discovery. I used my isolation as a canvas to paint the beginnings of a new chapter in my life. In the silence, I heard my inner voice whispering, guiding me to understand myself better.

I formed friendships with people from many backgrounds, drawn together by our similar experiences as strangers to a new place. My early friendships became a lifeline (or so I thought), providing support and company. At the same time, I handled the trials of my new existence.

Among the faces of my newfound friends, one gave me a surprising sense of comfort—a familiar face from my past. This unexpected encounter promised familiarity amid the unknown. It was a reminder that even in the most remote corners of the globe, strands of connection may weave through our lives.

The decision to move was a significant and life-altering choice. It was a journey that involved more than simply geographical movement; it necessitated a commitment to engage in a deep process of unlearning and relearning.

Coming to Ireland was not just a change of location but a total shift of perspective, culture, and manner of life. It was a process that forced me to unlearn preconceived assumptions, remove layers of cultural conditioning, and accept a new way of being.

Adapting to a new nation and culture is a subtraction process. It entails letting go of deeply rooted beliefs, biases, and habits that no longer serve us in this new context.

One of the most challenging problems I found during this unlearning process was confronting my preconceptions and prejudices. It's easy to bring cultural prejudices and misconceptions when entering a foreign society. However, I soon discovered these biases hindered my ability to fully engage with and comprehend people and situations.

Adapting to a new culture necessitates vulnerability—the willingness to leave one's comfort zone, ask questions, and make mistakes. It entails admitting that we don't have all the answers and that learning from others is essential.

Re-evaluating our priorities and values is also part of the unlearning process. Moving to a new country frequently entails experiencing new societal standards and expectations. What was important in one culture may be less critical in a different cultural setting. Accepting diversity and changing our values to fit our new surroundings are essential to unlearning and relearning.

Relearning, conversely, is the process of obtaining new knowledge and abilities specific to the unique culture and lifestyle. It necessitates a genuine interest in the host country's habits, traditions, and language. Relearning does not imply deleting one's identity but broadening it to include the richness of one's new cultural experience.

By assuming the best intentions in our encounters, we generate a spirit of goodwill and openness that can overcome cultural differences.

The value of humility is one of the most important lessons I've learned on this journey of unlearning and relearning. Adapting to a new country requires us to set aside our pride and adopt a humble attitude. It entails being open to advice and correction from people more familiar with the culture.

Making friends became a top priority in a city where I had no existing social groups: this required courage, openness, and a dash of luck.

My emotions were an intricate blend of excitement and apprehension as I embarked on this uncharted journey. My quest led me to Portarlington, a serene village in County Laois, Ireland. It was a place of undeniable beauty, not only in its picturesque landscapes but also in the inherent kindness of its residents. Choosing Portarlington as my new home turned out to be a stroke of brilliance, for I soon discovered that the people of Laois were among the most compassionate in all of Ireland.

In this welcoming community, I was fortunate to be among neighbours who epitomised the essence of support and unity. Among them was Fiachra, a gracious Irish neighbour who resided just across the street from my house. In his unceasing kindness, Fiachra meticulously tended to my lawns, a gesture that filled my heart with gratitude.

Another remarkable neighbour who quickly became a cherished ally was Lorcan. His warm-hearted nature and willingness to lend a helping hand made him an invaluable asset. Lorcan was always ready to run errands and assist my children and me, even at short notice. His unwavering commitment showcased the strong bonds that tied our community together.

In this charming corner of Ireland, I found a new place to call home and a neighbourhood that embodied the true spirit of neighbourly support. I felt immensely blessed to consider Portarlington my home, as most neighbours, like a piece of a welcoming puzzle, contributed to the intricate mosaic of my life in this remarkable community.

I arrived in Ireland at the end of January, and within seven months after my arrival, a series of events occurred that would forever alter the trajectory of my voyage. One of the most advantageous contacts I had during this time was reuniting with Sarah—a neighbour I had known since I was 17 in my college days in Enugu, Nigeria. The sight of her was like a ray of sunshine, and I thought it was a sign that God was ordering my steps. Unknown to me, this was the start of a new chapter in my life that would steer the wheel of fate in an undiscovered direction. It threw me through a never-ending series of challenges, exposing a web of deception and complex personalities that had previously lingered in the shadows of my existence.

During the tumult, my marriage's already frail links were put through a painful crucible, shaking its very foundation as the pressure increased. This became the looming test that would either shatter the feeble remains of our relationship or forge it anew in the fires of hardship.

Meeting someone from Nigeria who seemed to understand me, recognised our shared cultural nuances and shared my past was a huge source of comfort. It felt like a piece of home had found me in a faraway location, and I excitedly welcomed the chance to renew our friendship.

I approached this friendship with an open heart, wanting to provide the same support and kindness my newfound friend had shown me. Though she had been in the country before me, we continued to face the hurdles of adjusting to a new country together, and our friendship grew.

Meeting Sarah (not her real name) was a turning point in my path. Our paths initially crossed while we were both young students with big hopes. Sarah and I enjoyed a special kinship that transcended time and space now that we were together in Ireland.

Sarah's presence in my life during those early months of transition was nothing short of a blessing. She lived near my house, and our re-established connection grew swiftly. Her warmth, friendliness, and familiarity gave me comfort and a sense of belonging during considerable uncertainty.

Sarah was not just a friend but also a confidante. Our chats provided solace in times of homesickness and amusement in the face of cultural misunderstandings. She had gone through the difficulties of relocating and understood the emotional rollercoaster I was on.

Sarah was very supportive. She became my tour guide through the complexities of life in our new home, providing essential guidance on everything from using public transportation to comprehending the local language and registering my children in school. Her generosity knew no limitations, and she frequently extended invites to meetings and events, introducing me to her social circle.

Sarah taught me the value of reconnecting with someone from my past while also creating a more profound connection in the present. Our shared background enlivened our chats, and we nostalgically recalled our school days. We also honoured the people we had become, each moulded by our life experiences.

Sarah's friendship exemplified the enduring strength of human ties. It served as a reminder that friendship can provide the stability and support needed to navigate new seas even amid a significant life upheaval. Sarah was a consistent presence in my life over the months, a treasured companion on this transforming Journey.

Friendships are threads that weave together experiences, emotions, and shared moments in our lives. As support pillars, they may provide comfort, laughter, and a sense of belonging through change and transition. Unexpected circumstances and hidden motives can test even the most robust connections, leading to shifting tensions between friendship and betrayal.

Amid new beginnings, shadows of uncertainty can seep in, throwing doubt on the intentions of those we care about.

As my bond with Sarah grew, minor alterations began to surface. Our encounters were tinged with jealousy, and a once-solid bond began to reveal hairline cracks. So, I started deciphering indicators of a strained companionship and psychologically struggled to make sense of evolving dynamics.

This revelation was fraught with disillusionment, hurt, and bewilderment. The shock of discovering false information conveyed by this 'friend' sent a mix of fear and shockwaves to my perception of making friends and across my newly discovered support network.

The lessons uncovered challenged me to investigate the convolution of human emotions, trust's brittleness, and the unexpected nature of friendships. It served as a reminder that even the most honest relationships can be corrupted by hidden agendas and that our connections require caution and judgment.

Sarah's assistance was a lifeline in those early days, and I was overwhelmed with appreciation for her presence. I mistakenly assumed, perhaps foolishly, that her benevolence was evidence of a solid and sincere friendship. I saw her genuine affection for me and my children and hugged her like a long-lost sister.

She became an essential part of my life in many ways. Her steadfast support stretched beyond emotional relationships and into the details of our everyday lives. Recognising the necessity for mobility, I purchased a larger vehicle, an eight-seater, to comfortably accommodate her and our children. The apparent ease with which I managed this purchase led her to misconstrue my financial situation, believing it to be a product of my husband's wealth. Unbeknownst to her, this decision was a significant personal sacrifice undertaken solely to enhance our shared comfort. I had no idea that seeds of jealousy were growing. The warning signs of impending turbulence were initially minor and easily missed in light of our restored relationship.

These clues, though, would fester into something more substantial over time, affecting the direction of our relationship in unanticipated ways. Sarah's presence had offered a sense of security and familiarity to my life, for which I was glad.

The most incredible friendships can be torn apart. Once a source of comfort and strength, my connection with Sarah started to feel strained. We had loved harmony, but it seemed like an invisible storm was rising beneath the surface.

A particular incident vividly marked the beginning of a change in the dynamics of my friendship with Sarah. She had asked my children to fetch something from my room, but instead of immediately complying, they sought my permission first. Sarah's irritation at their consultation was palpable and led to a noticeable tension.

Curious about her reaction, I inquired about her feelings, only to be met with a comment that bewildered me. She remarked that my children acted like "Nigerian children," highlighting their habit of checking in with me before completing any errands she requested. This observation struck me as odd—after all, they were Nigerians, and seeking parental guidance seemed perfectly natural to me, irrespective of your nationality. I had indeed encouraged them to constantly seek my approval, a practice Sarah challenged, asserting that as a close friend, her requests should be heeded by my children within my home without my explicit consent. This was a stance I found myself unable to agree with.

In another telling incident, I had requested Sarah to look after my children while I ran an errand, and during this time, I phoned my children to check on them. To my surprise, my daughter needed to step outside to talk to me privately. This deviation from her usual, open behaviour was initially puzzling. It wasn't typical for her to seek privacy for such conversations, underscoring the significant shift in our relationship with Sarah. My daughter's actions spoke volumes about the evolving dynamics and the underlying tension that had begun to influence their interactions.

These instances were like pieces of a puzzle that I couldn't entirely fit together at the time. However, they were symptoms of a more significant problem boiling beneath the surface. They alluded to a developing uneasiness within Sarah, which appeared to be caused by my children's activities and conduct.

Jealousy is a complex emotion that generally stems from insecurity or a fear of being replaced or overshadowed. Sarah seemed to perceive my children's connection to me as a threat to what she would gain, which contradicted my understanding of our friendship. Her jealousy grew, and it looked like she was examining every part of our friendship, looking for reasons to feel threatened.

These were signs that our relationship was changing in unexpected ways. However, rather than tackling the fundamental issues at hand, I preferred to blame Sarah's actions as stress or temporary failures in judgment at this point.

It's easier in friendship, like in life, to ignore warning signs and your intuition and hope for the best. I was hesitant to acknowledge that the friendship I held dear might be on the verge of change, so, like the Irish saying, I grew long fingers and clung to the hope that our bond would weather the storm.

However, the storm was far from ending. The subtle hints of envy would soon become a turbulent force that would force me to confront the harsh truth of betrayal and the fragility of trust.

***

In the quiet of the early morning, an unexpected call from my husband broke the silence. He inquired about my whereabouts, to which I replied that I was at home. His questions persisted, probing whether I had travelled or was alone. I couldn't help but laugh, amused by the situation's absurdity, as solitude had become my constant companion.

However, my laughter did not resonate with him. Instead, it fuelled a more intense line of questioning. It became evident that his call was not rooted in casual conversation but out of suspicion and distrust. Perplexed by his interrogative tone, I felt compelled to ask why he was subjecting me to such an inquiry. He ignored my question and continued with his barrage of questions.

It's worth noting that at the time, communication between my husband and I had dwindled to a mere trickle when being "too busy" had become a regular refrain, and he expressed an inability to engage in video calls.

As the days passed, I couldn't shake the feeling that something was wrong. Whispers appeared to swirl through the air, casting doubt on the integrity of the connections I had made.

My cousin Shay provided the first indication of underhand activities at play when he revealed that a close friend in whom I had complete faith might have written a critical note addressed to my husband. His remarks sent ripples of worry through my mind.

Immediately, I began looking for hints to identify the name of the friend who had given this false information, when a familiar face came to mind-Sarah! She had once admitted to me to be meddling in the affairs of a married couple. Had she crossed the line here also?

The day of confrontation was a day of reckoning that revealed the truth hidden beneath layers of falsehood. It was a moment of unedited honesty and emotion, a collision of accusations and admissions that would permanently alter the trajectory of my life.

A rising mistrust that had festered within me like a festering wound was the catalyst for this confrontation. The devastating note, a toxic concoction of lies and distortions, had inspired an obsessive search for the truth in me. I had no hard evidence, only a nagging suspicion pointing to a source uncomfortably near home.

I set out on a disastrous voyage to confront Sarah; the friend turned foe who had re-entered my life in the most spiteful ways, with a heavy heart and a maelstrom of emotions rising within me. I knew she had the answers I sought and was determined to get them from her.

As I stood on her porch, ringing the bell that would signal the start of our confrontation, the air was packed with anxiety. I unleashed a barrage of inquiries and accusations when she opened the door. I confronted her with the apparent fact that she had sent that nasty note to my husband. This heinous act had ripped the fabric of our already frail relationship.

Her first reaction was a poor denial, an attempt to shift blame away from herself. Her boyfriend, an uninvited bystander in our argument, saw right through her ruse. He revealed her true nature, declaring that she was completely capable of such deception. It was a stunning admission that demolished any pretence of innocence she had.

In life, moments arrive that cleave time into before and after, etching their mark upon our memory with the clarity of etched glass. One such moment unfolded in Sarah's living room, a space that had once been a haven of friendship but had since transformed into a battleground of wills. It was there that Sarah, a woman whose calm demeanour I had always known, became the epicentre of a vehement tempest.

Sarah's genuine feelings erupted in a torrent of hate and venom at that tense moment. She agreed that she sent the note to my husband

and that she did it to get back at me for supporting my child over her when my child offended her. I even came to her house and spoke to her ominously. Her outburst was a mosaic of frustration, envy and anger. "I don't care!" she screamed. "If you wish to lord over others, return to Nigeria," she spat, the words laden with a venom that belied our shared history. This was not merely an argument but an unveiling of Sarah's rawest sentiments.

Though laced with hyperbole, her tirade held a mirror to my face, challenging me to see beyond my narrative and question the foundation of our disagreement. In her concluding words, likening me to "The Lord of the Rings," Sarah not only underscored the chasm between our perceptions but also marked the end of an era in our friendship, propelling me into a reflection on identity, privilege, and the intricate dance of cross-cultural navigation.

I was astonished and could not move. I came to accuse her, hoping she would deny she wasn't the one, but she could not stop talking. My mouth was left agape; I was in shock!

A startling insight washed over me as I listened to her remarks. This conversation was more than just exposing a liar; it reminded me of the irreparable schism that had grown in my marriage. My husband's inclination to accept her charges without inquiry and his willingness to believe the worst about me exposed the cracks in our marriage. It became evident that he was looking for a cause to end the relationship, and her lies gave an excellent justification.

My misgivings about our marriage's survival hardened into a terrible certainty at that time. The trust that had previously been the foundation of our relationship had been shattered, and there was no way back to the beautiful unity we had enjoyed. My marriage, which I had held onto for over a decade and a half, had disintegrated beneath the weight of betrayal and deception.

The encounter was a turning point in my path and clarified the confusion. It was a difficult but necessary step in acknowledging the truth of my circumstances and paving the way for a fresh start.

Her betrayal taught me about the obscurity of human nature, the complications of trust, and the power of resilience in the face of falsehood.

Sarah used Facebook as a channel for her evil intent, bombarding my husband with fabrications and half-truths. Words take on a life of their own in the digital realm, and the poison she wove seeped insidiously into the crevices of our already fragile relationship.

The timing was ominous. Our marriage was hanging by a thread, weighed down by unacknowledged disputes and unhealed traumas. Sarah's schemes took advantage of this vulnerability, making it all too easy for my husband to jump into the false narrative she portrayed. Our prior difficulties had already blurred reality, and the lies she spun were woven perfectly into the fabric of his perception.

The magnitude of her claims and the intricacies of her lies are shrouded in mystery. The profundity of her deceptions, the phrases that slithered from her computer to his screen, elude my understanding. I was left wrestling with the weight of the unknown, persistent questions that demanded answers, and a sense of betrayal that threatened to overwhelm me.

A new story emerged as the echoes of her deception resonated through our lives. Sarah's pernicious rumours soon emerged as a hideous distortion of my reality. I began to hear rumours that I had moved from Nigeria with a man, rumours that portrayed a scandalous picture of an affair. She also said there was no need to ask my children as they would do and say what I asked them to. These allegations were incorrect and ludicrous, having no basis in reality. There was no male in the picture and no illicit affair.

Her dark plot far exceeded her expectations. Poisoned by her remarks, my spouse avoided any direct communication with me. Instead of seeking an explanation or voicing his concerns, he chose to propagate these damaging charges to my family and friends. The ripple effect of her lies reached the shores of my extended family, casting doubt on my character and honesty.

These fabrications had far-reaching and devastating consequences. My cousins interrogated me nonstop, armed with the twisted version of events. They cast doubt on my decisions, actions, and motivations. The essence of my identity was called into question, destroying the trust I had built over a lifetime.

During the confusion and turbulence, I was battling a storm of emotions. The weight of false claims exacerbated my loneliness and isolation, leaving me adrift in a sea of doubt. The persistent assault on my character eroded my self-esteem, spreading seeds of doubt in the rich soil of my already fragile psyche.

I wasn't alone in this emotional storm. Even when the waves of despair threatened to consume me, the responsibilities of motherhood and the impending entrance of a new life required my attention. The weight of these responsibilities, in addition to the mental upheaval I was experiencing, generated a never-ending maelstrom within me.

The thought of escape took hold in my worst moments. The agony and isolation were too much for me, and I considered fleeing the hell that had become my reality. The agony of the situation drove me to the brink of suicide, and I contemplated suicide to escape the never-ending barrage of sorrow and betrayal.

For weeks, as my children left for school each day, I found myself sinking deeper into despair so profound that I sought refuge in a bottle of vodka, consuming a litre in the futile hope that it would bring an end to my unborn baby and my suffering before my other children returned from school.

One fateful day, I questioned the worth of it all in the darkest depths of my despair. Even if my husband had chosen to believe a stranger's words, what difference did it make? Even if I were carrying another man's child, did it diminish my right to life and happiness? Even if I had contemplated running away or starting anew with someone else, so what? If I die in all of this, my husband will probably be in the arms of another woman by the next day, and what happens to my children? The picture of a stepmother bringing up my children and maltreating them raced through my mind, and I grappled with the notion that ending my life seemed like the only way out. It was as if my life had lost all meaning, but it was not worth dying, mainly because of those who had never truly placed their trust in me. The only individuals who would bear the brunt of this unbearable pain were my innocent children, the very heartbeats of my existence. At that point, I knew I had to fight and live for them.

The most profound irritation in that entire ordeal wasn't rooted in humiliation, annoyance, or a sense of being deceived. Instead, the sting of betrayal resonated most deeply within me—heartbreak not solely at the hands of the man I was married to but also from someone I had once considered a true friend, and this moment marked a significant turning point, a crucible of despair that catalysed a transformative journey towards self-discovery and renewal.

In life's journey, losing sight of our worth is easy, especially when our roles as partners, mothers, or caretakers become all-encompassing. Heartbreaks, disappointments, betrayals, and periodic failures can lead to self-doubt, ultimately eroding one's confidence and casting shadows on personal growth and resilience. That was the new me.

In facing such challenges, it's crucial to embark on a journey of self-reflection and healing. Embrace support from loved ones, seek professional guidance if necessary, and engage in practices that foster mental and emotional well-being, such as mindfulness, journaling, and physical activity. Cultivating a mindset of growth and resilience, recognising your intrinsic worth, and setting achievable goals can also reignite the spark of confidence, guiding you back to a place of strength and self-assurance.

Lessons

The transformation of a friend into a foe is a profound and often painful experience, yet it's ripe with lessons about human nature, relationships, and personal growth. Here are vital lessons gleaned from such experiences:

- Trust is Precious: The experience teaches the value of trust and how it must be earned and given cautiously. Only some people who enter our lives will treat our trust with the respect it deserves.

- Intuition Matters: Subtle signs and gut feelings often indicate something is amiss. This experience underscores the importance of listening to and trusting our intuition about the people in our lives.

- Boundaries are Vital: It highlights the necessity of establishing and maintaining healthy boundaries in relationships. Clear boundaries can protect us from potential harm and disrespect.

- People Change: Friends turning into foes is a poignant reminder that people change over time. Their values, priorities, or life paths may differ, affecting the relationship dynamics.

- Resilience is Key: Navigating the betrayal teaches resilience. It shows that we can endure hurt and betrayal, learn from them, and emerge stronger.

- Self-Worth is Non-Negotiable: Such betrayals often prompt a reassessment of self-worth. They teach us that our value does not diminish because of someone else's inability to see it or their decision to betray our trust.

- Forgiveness is Liberating: Learning to forgive, especially when challenging, offers freedom. Forgiveness is more about liberating ourselves from the burden of bitterness than it is about absolving someone else's actions. Andy Stanley says, "In the shadow of my hurt, forgiveness feels like a decision to reward my enemy. But in the shadow of the cross, forgiveness is merely a gift from one undeserving soul to another."

- Letting Go and Moving On: The process teaches the importance of letting go of toxic relationships and moving forward. Holding onto resentment only poisons our well-being.
- The Power of Reflection: Reflecting on what went wrong and acknowledging any ignored red flags or contributions to the downfall can be enlightening and help prevent similar situations in the future.
- Value of True Friendships: Experiencing the pain of a friend's betrayal magnifies the value of genuine, trustworthy friendships. It teaches us to cherish and invest more in relationships with those who have proven themselves true friends.

While painful, transforming a friend into a foe imparts invaluable lessons that, if heeded, can lead to profound personal growth and more robust, more authentic relationships in the future.

Exercises

Recovering from betrayal, especially by someone close, can be an emotionally taxing process. However, engaging in specific exercises can facilitate healing, help manage the emotional turmoil, and guide you towards regaining trust in yourself and others. Here are several exercises designed to aid in your recovery after experiencing betrayal:

1. Journaling for Emotional Release

Exercise: Write down your feelings about the betrayal every day. Allow yourself to express anger, sadness, confusion, or any other emotions without judgment. Over time, shift your focus towards writing about your healing process and any insights you're gaining.

2. Letter Writing for Closure

Exercise: Write a letter to the person who betrayed you, expressing everything you feel. Detail how their actions affected you, what you wish had been different, and how you're choosing to move forward. Note: You don't need to send this letter. It's for your healing.

3. Visualization for Letting Go

Exercise: Close your eyes and visualise the person who betrayed you. Imagine a conversation where you tell them how you feel and ultimately say goodbye. Visualise yourself walking away, leaving the hurt behind and moving towards a bright, peaceful future.

4. Gratitude List to Shift Perspective

Exercise: Each day, write down three things you're grateful for. Try to include at least one thing related to your personal growth since the betrayal. This practice helps shift focus from loss to appreciation for what remains and what's been gained.

5. Self-Care Plan to Rebuild Trust in Yourself

Exercise: Create a weekly self-care plan that includes activities promoting physical, emotional, and mental well-being. Whether reading, taking walks, meditating, or spending time with supportive friends, prioritise actions that make you feel good about yourself.

6. *Social Support Circle*

Exercise: Identify people in your life who are supportive and trustworthy. Make efforts to spend time with them, share your feelings, and allow them to help you through this time. Building positive relationships helps counterbalance the effects of betrayal.

7. *Setting Boundaries Exercise*

Exercise: Reflect on the boundaries that were crossed, leading to betrayal. Write down what healthy boundaries look like for you in relationships. Practice setting these boundaries in your current and future relationships to protect yourself from similar hurt.

8. *Forgiveness Meditation*

Exercise: Engage in guided forgiveness meditations. Focus on forgiving yourself first for any self-blame related to the betrayal, then gradually work towards forgiving the betrayer if you choose. Forgiveness is for your peace and can be a powerful tool for healing.

9. *Professional Support*

Exercise: Consider seeking the support of a therapist or counsellor. They can offer personalised exercises and strategies to help you navigate your feelings, rebuild self-esteem, and develop a healthier outlook on relationships.

10. Creative Expression

Exercise: Use art, music, writing, or another form of creative expression to process your feelings. Creating something out of your experience can be a powerful way to understand and release your emotions.

Each of these exercises can play a crucial role in your journey from the pain of betrayal to a place of strength, healing, and eventual peace. Remember, healing is a process, and taking it one step at a time is okay.

CHAPTER 4

Reframing Regrets

"Regret looks back. Fear looks around. Worry looks in. Faith looks up."

- Nicky Gumbel.

In my pursuit of truth and reconciliation, I contacted my cousin Shay, who first brought the distressing rumours to my attention. I shared the revelations I had uncovered with him. I expressed my deep-seated anguish regarding the situation and how much I regretted my marriage—the time had come to dissolve the bonds of the marriage. There appeared to be no merit in clinging to a facade of normalcy. If my husband could give credence to fabrications spun by an outsider, it signified the absence of trust, which is the cornerstone of any marriage. In such a scenario, persevering with the union felt futile, as its foundation had crumbled.

Shay, embodying the role of a sage, counselled patience and urged me to seek a resolution before taking drastic measures. Heeding his advice, I embarked on a journey to mend the fractures within my family. I reached out to my uncles, extended family members, and anyone else who were influenced by the rumours that loomed over my existence. The process was a humbling ordeal, during which I issued apologies repeatedly as I narrated the truth of my circumstances. To my relief, my family welcomed my candidness and apologies, which I extended on behalf of both my husband and myself for any distress caused. Their overall reaction was sympathetic and understanding, with soothing words for the trauma I had been through. They showed support and requested that I contact the man Sarah had wrongly accused of being my boyfriend. Their offer of support and forgiveness was a gesture that underscored the enduring bonds of family and the healing power of understanding.

The most critical step forward in restoring trust came when the man whose name had been pulled into this web of deception was found. The truth carried its weight, as it often does. This individual, who was supposed to be the boyfriend in question, turned out to be someone completely unrelated to the rumours. He was financially secure, content with his family, and far apart from the contrived story.

The unravelling of this elaborate deception network marks a defining moment in my path. Torn between worry and confusion rebuilding trust with my family became a more attainable goal. The truth had the potential to heal the wounds caused by lies and gossip, and it was the first step in reclaiming the ties I had feared had been gone forever.

Each thread of life experience, whether dyed in the vibrant hues of joy or the sober tones of sorrow, contributes to the masterpiece that is our existence. As we navigate through relationships and encounters, we inevitably come across corridors darkened by gossip and betrayal. It is in these shadowed halls where the seeds of regret may find fertile ground, sprouting bitter reflections on why paths crossed and fates intertwined.

Encountering individuals whose actions wound the spirit can anchor us in a vortex of regret, prompting us to lament the day of the meeting. Yet, dwelling in the echo chamber of what-ifs and should-haves is a Sisyphean task that only compounds our suffering, chaining us to a past that can neither be altered nor forgotten. Instead, this chapter advocates for the alchemy of perspective, urging you to transmute the leaden weight of regret into the gold of personal growth.

Rather than cataloguing losses and nursing grievances, we explore the empowerment found in forward motion. This healing comes from using our time and energy not to excavate the ruins of disappointment but to construct the towers of a brighter, more resilient self. Through the exercises shared within these pages, you will discover how moving on is not merely a physical departure from the sources of our pain but a deliberate choice to enrich and elevate our inner lives.

Guilt and shame are powerful emotions that can trap us in a web of self-doubt and regret, particularly when experiencing the aftermath of a relationship's end or realising lost time in unfulfilling roles. The key is to shift your mindset from self-blame to self-compassion while enabling a journey towards healing and self-acceptance.

Before we can transcend these emotions, we must first understand them. Guilt is the feeling that arises when we believe we have done something wrong, while shame goes deeper, suggesting that we are bad at our core. Both are rooted in the expectations we set for ourselves and those imposed by society, often leaving us feeling trapped in a cycle of self-criticism.

For healing to commence, I had to confront my most profound regret: the haunting spectre of lost time. Rather than dwelling in the shadows of ancient moments, I chose a transformative path forward—education. As I embarked on this academic odyssey, uncertainty clouded my every step. Past missteps had shaken my confidence and eroded my judgment. The daunting prospect of navigating uncharted territories without a clear direction and the doubt I had in my decision-making abilities weighed heavily upon me.

Despite these tumultuous waves of doubt, an undeniable truth offered a beacon of light: the pursuit of knowledge is a path devoid of missteps. Engaging in the quest for learning guaranteed that, regardless of the outcomes, I would emerge enriched and armoured with wisdom and insight. This conviction illuminated the way forward, transforming my apprehension into a wellspring of courage. I recognised that embracing education was not merely a safe harbour but a venture brimming with potential—a risk imbued with the promise of personal growth and enlightenment.

This deliberate shift in perspective, from lamenting lost time to valuing the pursuit of knowledge, marked a pivotal chapter in my saga. It was a testament to the power of reframing regrets, not as anchors that tether us to our past failures but as stepping stones towards a future bright with the prospects of wisdom and fulfilment. In embracing this journey, I discovered that true wisdom lies in recognising that every step taken in the pursuit of knowledge is a step towards liberating oneself from the chains of regret and moving closer to bliss.

This significant shift in focus experienced along the way to achieving personal growth and independence was what set me on the path to higher learning, professional advancement, and self-improvement. It was an enlightening voyage propelled by the conviction that, in the wise words of Nelson Mandela, "Education is the most powerful weapon which you can use to change the world."

From a very young age, the importance of education was a principle deeply ingrained in me by my parents. They often spoke of it not just as a pathway to opportunity but as the one possession that remains inviolable, the treasure that no one could ever strip away from me. This foundational belief became the bedrock upon which I built my aspirations. With a heart full of determination and a mind eager for exploration, I embarked on a quest for knowledge, viewing each lesson learned as a precious stone added to the fortress of my future. Education became a source of hope for me, blazing a way to a brighter future.

My dedication to knowledge went beyond personal enrichment; it was also a means of breaking free from constraints because When you know better, you do better. Armed with information, I felt empowered to make informed decisions and build my path to freedom.

Pursuing career advancement was the next essential stage in the unfolding narrative of my transforming journey. I searched for possibilities aligned with my interests and values. Each career change brought me closer to the elusive worlds of self-actualisation and financial independence.

Personal growth and transformation frequently necessitate the fortitude to venture into unknown territory, challenge the status quo, and welcome change as an opportunity for self-reinvention. For me, this transforming journey expressed itself in the transitions between careers.

Drawing upon a diverse array of professional experiences spanning banking, telecommunications, retail, and business development, complemented by a degree in Engineering, extensive project management expertise, and a multitude of certifications garnered worldwide; I entered the job market in Ireland with a sense of confidence. However, I soon encountered an unexpected hurdle after several months of job search: the elusive requirement of "Irish experience" that seemed to overshadow my qualifications.

Realising the importance of establishing a professional identity in a new environment while also providing for my family, I made a strategic decision. I recognised that swift entry into the workforce and financial stability were paramount. With this in mind, I pivoted towards a career path offering immediate opportunities for employment and growth.

Healthcare support emerged as the logical choice—an industry renowned for its abundant job prospects and a field where some of my skills acquired from St. Angela's Nursing Home and Maternity could be readily applied. In embracing this new direction, I embarked on a journey to forge a meaningful career trajectory that would provide financial security and pave the way for a fulfilling start of professional identity in Ireland.

I registered for a Fetac level 5 support in healthcare training and started my work experience alongside it, and in a few months, I had graduated and was earning money.

I spent two years as a healthcare assistant, nurturing a growing ambition and an unwavering commitment to personal advancement. It became abundantly clear that I yearned for more substantial challenges and sought opportunities to channel my skills and experience into a more fulfilling professional trajectory.

With a deep reservoir of knowledge and an unrelenting desire to contribute, I reached a pivotal juncture in my Journey where I decided to transition to IT (Information Technology). Determined to chart a new course, I recognised that to maximise my potential and establish my professional identity in IT; I needed to learn new skills and gain new knowledge. This understanding led me back to the hallowed halls of academia, where I began my quest to be educated in IT networks and infrastructure at Dublin Business School. It was a significant adjustment that demanded both vision and determination.

In life, our passions and interests are the vibrant threads that add colour and texture, transforming the mundane into something extraordinary. Let us embark on a short, reflective journey where I am inviting you to explore, discover, ignite your curiosity, and pursue the activities that bring you joy and fulfilment. It's about recognising that personal growth is not a destination but a journey enriched by pursuing our passions.

Begin by asking yourself what activities make you lose track of time, what topics you could read about for hours, or what you daydream about doing. These are clues to your passions. For some, this may be a straightforward process, while for others, it may require deeper self-exploration. Allow yourself the freedom to explore without judgment. Remember, passions are not limited to artistic pursuits; they can be found in any domain that resonates with you.

One barrier to pursuing our interests is the need for more time or space in our daily lives. Make a conscious effort to carve out time for exploration. This might mean setting aside a specific time each week to try something new or dedicating a small portion of your day to a hobby. Approach this time with a sense of curiosity and play. The goal is not to achieve mastery (that comes with time) but to allow yourself the joy of discovery.

Adopt a beginner's mind as you explore new interests. In this mindset, there are no mistakes, only learning opportunities. It's about embracing the process without being overly concerned with the outcome. Remember, every expert was once a beginner. The willingness to be a novice, to make mistakes, and to learn from them is a crucial part of growth and discovery.

Seek out communities or groups that share your interests. This could be a local club, an online forum, or a class. Connecting with others who share your passions can provide motivation, inspiration, and support. It's also an excellent way to make new friends and expand your social circle.

As you become more involved in your new interest, consider setting specific goals related to your passion. This could involve completing a project, achieving a certain skill level, or even sharing your passion with others. Setting goals can provide direction and a sense of purpose within your pursuit.

Look for ways to integrate your passions into your daily life. This doesn't mean you need to turn your hobby into a career (though, for some, this might be a dream come true). Instead, it's about allowing your passions to influence your life positively, whether through the joy they bring, the people they introduce you to, or the balance they provide to your work and responsibilities.

Pursuing your passions and interests is vital to personal growth and happiness. It's about allowing yourself to explore, learn, and engage deeply with the world around you. Your passions reflect your inner self, and by honouring them, you keep your uniqueness and potential. So, let curiosity be your guide, embrace the journey of discovery, and allow your passions to lead you toward a more fulfilling and vibrant life.

Self-improvement became my constant companion on this path. Personal development was a continuous process rather than a destination. I developed resilience, flexibility, and a growth mentality to overcome obstacles.

When the road to self-actualisation and independence seemed impossible, I thought of Eleanor Roosevelt's advice: "You gain strength, courage, and confidence by every experience in which you stop to look fear in the face. You must do the thing you think you cannot do." These remarks reminded me that facing challenges requires courage.

As I pursued education, career development, and self improvement, my life experiences have sharpened my thoughts and mindset, giving me the strength to face challenges, seize chances, and live a life aligned with my goals and desires.

Finally, I've realised the enormous influence of the emphasis on focus shift, adaptability and flexibility on my life. It wasn't simply about gaining knowledge, moving up the corporate ladder, or achieving personal progress. It was a voyage of self-discovery, empowerment, and transformation, allowing me to live a life of meaning, freedom, and fulfilment.

Lessons

- Regrets Can Become Catalysts for Change: Understanding that regrets can spur us to make positive changes is crucial. They are not merely reminders of what we did wrong but signals pointing us towards what we can do right in the future.
- The Power of Perspective: Learning to see past mistakes not as irreversible errors but as invaluable lessons helps transform our outlook on life and fosters growth.
- Embracing Forgiveness: Forgiving ourselves is a vital step in moving past regrets. Holding onto self-blame hinders progress, while forgiveness opens the door to healing and growth.
- Action Over Rumination: Dwelling on regrets without action can trap us in a cycle of negativity. Taking proactive steps towards change is essential for moving forward.
- The Importance of Present-Mindedness: Focusing on the present moment rather than past regrets or future anxieties teaches us the value of mindfulness in healing and happiness.
- Resilience Through Reflection: Reflecting on our regrets and the circumstances around them can build resilience, empowering us to face future challenges with strength and grace.
- Learning to Let Go: Understanding that some aspects of the past cannot be changed allows us to let go of deep-seated regrets and embrace the future with open arms.
- The Continuous Nature of Learning: Recognizing that learning is a lifelong journey helps us appreciate each experience, including our regrets, as opportunities for personal development.

- Finding Purpose in Pain: Sometimes, our greatest regrets lead us to discover our true passions and purposes in life, guiding us towards more fulfilling paths.
- The Strength in Vulnerability: Acknowledging and sharing our regrets can be a powerful tool for connection, healing, and helping others learn from our experiences, highlighting the strength found in vulnerability.
- Growth Over Guilt: By shifting focus from guilt to growth, we learn to view our life experiences as opportunities for personal development rather than moments of failure.
- Letting Go Liberates: One crucial lesson is that letting go of what cannot be changed frees up emotional and mental space for the new, the hopeful, and the transformative.
- Future Focused: Reframing regrets teaches us to invest our energy into future possibilities rather than dwelling on past impossibilities.
- Self-Compassion is Key: Through this process, we learn the importance of treating ourselves with kindness and understanding, recognising that self-criticism hinders growth.
- Decision-Making Confidence: By understanding that every choice, even seemingly wrong ones, leads to growth, we gain confidence in our decision-making abilities.
- Embrace Uncertainty: Reframing regrets encourages us to embrace uncertainty as a natural and beneficial aspect of life, fostering resilience and adaptability.
- Pathway to Peace: Ultimately, reframing regrets guides us toward inner peace, showing that acceptance and perspective shift can heal old wounds and create a foundation for a blissful future.

Exercises

Exercise 1 - Reframing Regret

Reframing regret is a powerful exercise for personal growth and healing. This activity aims to transform your view of past regrets into opportunities for learning and self-improvement. Follow these steps to practice reframing your regrets:

Step 1: Identify a Regret

Write down a specific regret you have, something that often comes to mind and affects your emotional state. Be as detailed as necessary to capture the situation and your feelings about it thoroughly.

Step 2: Acknowledge Your Feelings

Acknowledge and write down all the emotions associated with this regret—sadness, guilt, anger, etc. Recognising these feelings is crucial in understanding their impact on your life.

Step 3: Seek the Lessons

For every regret, there's a hidden lesson. Reflect on what this regret taught you or can teach you. Did it make you stronger? More empathetic? Did it reveal something about your values or desires? Write these insights down.

Step 4: Visualize an Alternate Outcome

Imagine how you would have preferred the situation to unfold. Visualising an alternative scenario can help you identify what was missing or what you truly desired at that moment.

Step 5: Plan for the Future

Using the lessons learned, outline how you can apply this knowledge in future situations. This might include how you'll approach similar challenges differently or how you can prevent a similar regret from forming.

Step 6: Transform the Narrative

Rewrite the story of your regret, focusing on the positive outcomes and lessons learned. This new narrative should empower you, highlighting growth, resilience, and the proactive steps you'll take moving forward.

Step 7: Share or Reflect

If comfortable, share this new narrative with a trusted friend or therapist. Sometimes, speaking it aloud or having it witnessed by another can reinforce the reframed perspective. If you prefer, simply reflecting on this new story can also be powerful.

Step 8: Create a Reminder

Craft a small reminder of this exercise's positive outcome—a note, a symbolic object, or even a mantra derived from your new narrative. Let this serve as a touchstone for when past regrets attempt to resurface.

Step 9: Practice Gratitude

Finally, practice gratitude for the growth and insights gained from this experience. Recognise the strength and wisdom you've drawn from navigating past regrets.

Step 10: Repeat as Needed
Reframing regret is an ongoing process. Repeat this exercise as new regrets surface or as you find yourself dwelling on past mistakes.

This exercise is not about denying past mistakes or regrets but transforming them into stepping stones for personal growth and a more fulfilling life.

Exercise 2 - Affirmations of Worth

Create a list of affirmations that reinforce your worth. These can be simple statements like, "I am worthy of love and respect," or more specific affirmations based on your strengths and achievements. Repeat these affirmations to yourself, especially during moments of doubt or self-criticism. Affirmations are powerful tools in rewiring our perceptions of ourselves, reminding us of our inherent worth.

Exercise 3 - Practicing Mindfulness and Self-Compassion

The Compassionate Observer

Set aside a few minutes each day to practice mindfulness. Sit quietly and observe your thoughts, especially those that trigger guilt or shame. Instead of engaging with these thoughts, imagine you are a compassionate observer. Acknowledge the thoughts, then gently remind yourself, "I am learning and growing." This practice encourages a kinder, more forgiving perspective towards oneself.

Exercise 4 - Reframing the Narrative

The Letter of Forgiveness

Write a letter to yourself about the situations that have caused you guilt or shame. Instead of focusing on blame, frame these experiences as opportunities for growth. Conclude the letter with words of forgiveness and understanding. This exercise helps in reframing the narrative from one of self-blame to one of learning and forgiveness.

Exercise 5 - Seeking Support and Sharing Your Story

The Power of Sharing

Sharing your feelings of guilt and shame with a trusted friend, family member, or therapist can be incredibly healing. Verbalising these emotions helps to diminish their power, providing a new perspective and the realisation that you are not alone in your experiences. Remember, seeking support is a sign of strength, not weakness.

Exercise 6 - Cultivating Gratitude and Positive Reflection

Daily Gratitude Journal

Daily, write down three things you are grateful for about yourself—qualities, actions, or moments of joy. This practice shifts the focus from what you perceive you've done wrong to the positive aspects of yourself and your life, fostering a sense of gratitude and self-appreciation.

Moving from self-blame to self-compassion is not a linear journey; it requires patience, practice, and persistence. By employing these strategies, you begin to loosen the grip of guilt and shame, paving the way for a relationship with yourself grounded in kindness, understanding, and unconditional self-love. Remember, the path to overcoming these emotions is through gentle acknowledgement, compassionate reflection, and the continuous practice of self-compassion.

Building Self-Esteem

Self-esteem is the foundation upon which we build a life of fulfilment, resilience, and joy. Our internal compass guides us through life's challenges and successes. Building self-esteem is not just about feeling good about ourselves—it's about recognising our inherent worth, respecting ourselves, and nurturing self-love. This section offers practical tips for enhancing self-esteem and fostering a relationship with yourself rooted in love and respect.

Tips

Tip 1: Set Achievable Goals - Actionable Steps for Goal Setting

Begin by setting small, achievable goals that align with your values and aspirations. These should be specific, measurable, attainable, relevant, and time-bound (SMART). Achieving these goals will provide a sense of accomplishment and reinforce your belief in your abilities. Celebrate these achievements, no matter how small, as each success builds upon your self-esteem.

Tip 2: Practice Positive Self-Talk

The Mirror Affirmation

Every morning, stand in front of the mirror and offer yourself words of encouragement and affirmation. Replace negative thoughts with positive ones. For instance, change "I can't do this" to "I can tackle challenges one step at a time." This exercise helps rewire your brain to focus on your strengths and potential rather than your perceived flaws or failures.

Tip 3: Cultivate Self-Compassion
The Loving-Kindness Practice

Engage in a daily practice of loving-kindness meditation. Focus on directing feelings of love, kindness, and compassion towards yourself. Repeat phrases such as "May I be happy, may I be healthy, may I be free from suffering." This practice helps cultivate a compassionate relationship with oneself, essential for building self-esteem.

Tip 4: Surround Yourself with Positive Influence
Evaluating Your Circle

Take a moment to evaluate the people in your life. Surround yourself with individuals who uplift, support, and encourage you. Limit your time with those who drain your energy or diminish your sense of self-worth. The company you keep significantly impacts your self-esteem, so choose relationships that foster positivity and growth.

Tip 5: Engage in Activities That Make You Feel Good
Finding Joy and Confidence

Identify activities that bring you joy and a sense of accomplishment. Whether it's a creative pursuit, physical activity, or a new hobby, engaging in activities you love can significantly boost your self-esteem. These activities provide a sense of achievement and help you connect with your passions and interests.

Tip 6: Reflect on Your Accomplishments

The Achievement Log

Keep a journal of your accomplishments, big or small. Reflecting on your achievements can boost confidence and remind you of your capabilities. This log serves as a tangible reminder of your strengths and successes, especially during moments of doubt or low self-esteem.

Building self-esteem is a journey of recognising and celebrating your worth, challenging negative self-perceptions, and embracing your uniqueness with kindness and compassion. By implementing these practical tips, you embark on a stronger, more loving relationship with yourself. Remember, self-esteem blooms from consistent self-love, positive self-talk, and surrounding yourself with uplifting influences. As you cultivate these practices, watch your self-esteem and self-love flourish, empowering you to live your most authentic and fulfilling life.

CHAPTER 5

Navigating the Blisters

"Doubt kills more dreams than failure ever will."

- Suzy Kassem.

Rebuilding trust is difficult, particularly when a web of deception and betrayal has shattered it. The path back to trust began with a critical revelation that revealed the truth hidden beneath layers of vicious rumours and false charges.

I was left with an intense disillusionment after my confrontation with Sarah. The idea that someone I had implicitly trusted had played a crucial part in spreading damaging lies about me was a difficult pill to swallow. It had shattered the foundations of my faith in others, leaving me to deal with the fallout from her deception.

Despite the chaos and heartbreak, a spark of optimism appeared. The unravelling of the rumours resulted in an unexpected revelation. The person she had mentioned as my boyfriend did not fit her description. It became clear that her story about a new man in my life was based on lies and misinformation. This revelation was a breakpoint that questioned the integrity of her entire story.

False claims spread like wildfire, casting shadows of suspicion over me. My close-knit community had become a breeding ground for gossip, and my name was on everyone's lips. I was portrayed as the protagonist of a story I had not written, and the weight of these lies weighed heavily on me.

Loneliness is a terrible foe that stole into my life like an unexpected intruder. The loneliness of being in a different country with no support system or familiar faces was difficult at first but bearable. However, the cacophony of rumours and the emotional anguish they caused heightened my sense of anxiety.

The continued conversation of society, rife with judgment and speculation, created an impassable barrier between me and the sense of belonging I craved. I retreated deeper into my thoughts, burdened by the weight of mistrust surrounding me, all the while trying to take care of my children and prepare for the imminent birth of my fourth child. Being pregnant under these conditions was a double-edged sword. While it represented new beginnings and promise, it also heightened my stress and mental anguish.

Caring for my children was both a blessing and a challenge. Their innocence and steadfast devotion gave me courage, but they were also acutely aware of the stress around us. Their inquiries about the rumours and my marriage felt like repeated piercings through my heart, where I walked a fine line between shielding them from the painful truths and being open about our situation.

My physical and emotional well-being became increasingly important as the pregnancy proceeded. I had to muster every ounce of strength I had to bear the weight of my children's future and hope for a better tomorrow.

The psychological toll of wrongly accusing someone is well documented. Psychological studies shed light on the emotional pain felt by people who are the target of false rumours or charges. A hint of wrongdoing can elicit guilt, embarrassment, and self-doubt, all of which nibble at one's self-esteem and emotional well-being.

In my instance, the allegations cut to the core of my identity as a mother and a woman. I was portrayed as a pregnant married woman who had relocated with another man who was living off me, a story that bore no reference to my reality. These claims had a severe emotional impact on me, instilling a sense of impotence and frustration as I wrestled with the realisation that I was being judged based on lies. My self-esteem and confidence, which were on a decline as a result of my failing relationship, deepened.

As the false charges spread throughout the community, I began to feel increasingly isolated. People who used to welcome me with warmth and kindness now looked at me with distrust and judgment. This social separation, both subtle and overt, exacerbated my loneliness.

Isolation, particularly during times of emotional hardship, has been shown in research to worsen symptoms of sadness and anxiety. My emotional well-being deteriorated as I dealt with the difficulties of pregnancy.

During this period, I had successfully secured residency to remain in the country; however, I could not have this vital status endorsed in my passport due to the absence of my children's passports, a necessary condition for completing the process. The disappearance of these documents was particularly alarming, leading me to suspect theft. Given that Sarah was the only individual aside from my family with access to our home, suspicion naturally gravitated towards her. Faced with this predicament, the alternative was to declare the passports missing and initiate an application for replacements. This procedure demanded the collective agreement of both my spouse and myself. Regrettably, my husband declined to provide his portion of the consent, citing his inability to visit the embassy owing to his busy schedule. This refusal effectively immobilised me, barring me from employment and restricting my ability to engage in most activities for over seven months. The proliferation of rumours exacerbated my sense of isolation and powerlessness, casting a shadow over this challenging phase of my life.

Pregnancy is a period when maternal mental health is critical, not only for the mother's well-being but also for the health of the unborn child. Rumours and false claims can cause stress, which can harm physical and psychological health. According to research, stress during pregnancy might contribute to issues like preterm birth and low birth weight.

The emotional weight I carried as I stood on the verge of motherhood was palpable. The tension caused by the rumours threatened not only my health but also the health of my unborn child. This new layer of worry added to the emotional strain I was already feeling.

I faced the painful reality that gossip and false accusations had become unwelcome companions on my odyssey to emotional healing and self-discovery. These bogus charges had the emotional impact of a hefty anchor, threatening to draw me beneath the stormy waters of despair. But amid difficulty, I discovered resilience and an unwavering commitment to safeguard my well-being and my children's future.

I found myself battling with the mounting burden of loneliness and the subtle seeds of psychological self-doubt as the days moved into weeks and weeks into months. My emotional path had taken an unexpected turn, sending me into unfamiliar terrain where solitude and uncertainty reigned supreme.

They claim that loneliness can be the most deafening stillness. It wasn't simply the physical distance from familiar individuals and places that made me feel lonely; it was also the terrible sense of being misunderstood and misjudged.

Loneliness has an odd way of increasing one's inner doubts and insecurities. In the seclusion of my new life, I was troubled by persistent questions: Was I correct to go on this journey? Could I truly recover from the wounds of my past? Were the charges levelled against me a mirror of some buried truth I refused to confront?

Psychological self-doubt, frequently prompted by external causes such as social isolation or criticism, can destroy one's self-esteem and self-worth. In my situation, the continuous rumours and social ostracisation that followed reinforced a sense of self-doubt that was difficult to overcome.

Balancing the emotional load of loneliness and self-doubt while caring for my children and being pregnant was a daunting task.

During times of emotional distress, psychologists frequently emphasise the value of social support. In my case, I was not only physically separated from my support network, but I was also dealing with the deterioration of my social support because of the rumours. My "closest friend" at the time told me she could not be seen as my friend anymore because she was still married and her husband would not like her alliance with me. This double-edged sword of isolation exacerbated my emotional weight.

Pregnancy is an emotional journey that includes physical changes, hormone imbalances, and increased susceptibility. It's a moment when a woman's emotional well-being can be incredibly delicate, and she desperately needs care and understanding.

As days passed by, it became clear that coping with this emotional load was about more than just surviving; it was also essential to protect my mental and emotional well-being for the sake of my children and the new life growing within me.

In her book "Postpartum Depression for Dummies," Psychologist Dr. Shoshana Bennett emphasises the need to seek help and control stress throughout pregnancy. She emphasises that the mother's emotional health has a direct impact on the developing foetus; thus, it is critical to address any emotional issues that arise.

Balancing the emotional burden while caring for my children and being pregnant was, without a doubt, one of the most challenging parts of my odyssey. It was, nevertheless, a time of great self-discovery and resilience. I realised the significance of parents. Oh, how I missed my mum and my dad!

Dr. Susan David, a psychologist and author noted for her work on emotional agility, emphasises the necessity of recognising and negotiating complex emotions. She also believes confronting and resolving challenging emotions can boost resilience and well-being.

Adopting a growth mindset is foundational to resilience. It's the belief that your abilities and intelligence can be developed through dedication and hard work. When faced with a setback, remind yourself of what you haven't mastered "yet" rather than what you can't do. This simple shift in language—from "I can't" to "I can't yet"—opens the door to growth and learning.

Human beings are inherently social creatures, and the quality of our connections with others significantly enhances our well-being. Creating a supportive network of friends, family, and professionals is beneficial and essential for our emotional and psychological health.

Lessons

In modern life, self-care emerges not as a luxury but as an indispensable foundation for cultivating resilience. This practice involves a conscientious approach to nurturing one's physical and emotional well-being, encompassing healthy dietary habits, regular exercise, sufficient rest, and engaging in stress-related activities, such as meditation and yoga. When our physical and emotional needs are attentively met, we are better equipped to manage stress and rebound from challenges gracefully.

The journey towards personal growth and healing intricately weaves through self-care and wellness. These elements are not mere milestones but constitute the path itself. By dedicating ourselves to practices that foster our well-being, we unlock the ability to rise above adversity, fortify our resilience, and achieve a harmonious life marked by balance and contentment.

Self-care is characterised by a deliberate effort to safeguard or enhance one's health, representing a vow to satisfy one's physical, emotional, and mental necessities. This practice is a testament to self-respect, ensuring that we are in the best possible state for ourselves and those around us. It transcends selfishness, deeply acknowledging our worth and responsibility to our well-being.

The pillars of physical health, such as engaging in regular exercise, maintaining a nutritious diet, ensuring adequate sleep, and staying hydrated, play a pivotal role in influencing our emotional and mental states. Physical activity, for instance, serves as a potent catalyst for physical fitness and triggers the release of endorphins, which mitigate stress and enhance mood. Similarly, the food we consume and our food chemistry influence our energy levels and emotional equilibrium.

Addressing mental and emotional wellness entails adopting practices that either maintain or improve mental health, including stress management, emotion regulation, and the cultivation of a positive mindset. Techniques like mindfulness meditation, deep breathing exercises, and journaling are invaluable for navigating stress and emotional turmoil. Furthermore, seeking professional assistance, be it through therapy or counselling, is a critical aspect of preserving mental health.

Establishing a routine that incorporates self-care practices lends a sense of stability and continuity, particularly in times of stress or transition. Such routines anchor, providing a structured backdrop for healing and growth. Whether it entails a morning exercise regimen, scheduled meals, or a nightly ritual, these practices foster a sense of order and contribute to overall well-being.

Central to the concept of self-care is the ethos of self-compassion and acceptance, acknowledging that healing is a journey marked by patience, gentleness, and the recognition that progress is seldom linear. Approaching oneself with the same compassion and empathy one would extend to a friend, acknowledging one's strengths, forgiving oneself for missteps, and celebrating every bit of progress, no matter how minor, are integral to the self-care journey.

Self-care and wellness are critical to the healing journey, offering a holistic approach to transforming life with resilience, fulfilment, and well-being. The path to healing is not about reaching a predetermined destination but nurturing ourselves at every step. By prioritising physical and mental health, establishing supportive routines, fostering positive relationships, and practising self-compassion, we lay the groundwork for a life rich in healing and growth.

Setting and working toward achievable goals fosters a sense of accomplishment and purpose. Break larger goals into smaller, manageable tasks, and celebrate each milestone. This practice moves you forward and reinforces your ability to overcome challenges and succeed.

View setbacks not as insurmountable failures but as valuable feedback. Ask yourself, "What can I learn from this experience?" This perspective encourages a proactive approach to challenges, turning obstacles into opportunities for growth and improvement.

Practicing gratitude can significantly enhance resilience. By focusing on what you're thankful for, you shift your perspective from what's lacking to what's abundant in your life. This shift fosters positive emotions and a greater sense of well-being, making it easier to navigate difficult times.

Exercise

Here are some practical tips that helped me build and nurture vital connections, ensuring a robust support system:

- Start by investing time and energy in your relationships with friends and family. These connections offer a bedrock of emotional support, understanding, and love. Prioritise regular check-ins, shared activities, and open communication. Remember that it is not the quantity of your social interactions that matters most, but the quality. Deep, meaningful connections provide a sense of belonging and support that can sustain you through life's ups and downs.
- While longstanding relationships are invaluable, expanding your social circle is also beneficial. However, tread with caution and limit exposures.
- Engage in activities and hobbies that interest you, whether joining a club, attending workshops, or volunteering. These settings provide natural opportunities to meet people with

similar interests, potentially leading to new friendships and connections.

- Seek professional support when needed: Sometimes, the support we need goes beyond what friends and family can offer. Therapists, counsellors, and life coaches can provide professional guidance, helping you navigate challenges, gain insights into your behaviour and emotions, and develop coping strategies. Don't hesitate to seek out these professionals; doing so is a sign of strength and a proactive step toward mental wellness.

- Many communities offer resources designed to support individuals through various life challenges. These can include support groups, educational workshops, and seminars on mental health and personal development. These resources provide valuable information and strategies and connect you with others facing similar situations, expanding your support network.

- In today's digital age, support networks extend beyond physical presence. Online forums, social media groups, and virtual meetups can provide community and support from the comfort of your home. These platforms allow for sharing experiences, advice, and encouragement across geographical boundaries, offering a unique and valuable form of support.

- Building a support network is not a one-time task but an ongoing process. Nurture your relationships through active engagement, empathy, and reciprocity. Be there for others as they are for you, offering your support, listening ear, and presence. Remember, the strength of your support network is not just in its existence but in the quality of mutual care and support.

Remember, no one is an island, and with a strong support network, you are better equipped to face whatever comes your way.

Resilience involves the ability to approach problems with strategic thinking. When faced with a challenge, take a step back to assess the situation, identify possible solutions, and develop an action plan. This approach empowers you to tackle problems head-on, reducing feelings of helplessness and stress.

Change is a constant in life, and resilience requires flexibility and adaptability. Embrace change as an opportunity for growth and remain open to new experiences and perspectives. This adaptability ensures you can pivot in response to life's uncertainties, maintaining your path toward your goals despite the changing landscape.

Developing resilience is a dynamic and ongoing process. It's about cultivating a mindset and set of practices that enable you to face life's challenges with courage and grace. By embracing these strategies, you'll build your capacity to withstand adversity and discover a more profound sense of purpose, fulfilment, and strength. Remember, resilience isn't about avoiding the storm but learning to dance in the rain.

Tips

25 ways to build Resilience

Building resilience is essential for navigating life's challenges effectively. Here are 25 tips to develop and build your resilience:

1. **Maintain Strong Relationships:** Cultivate supportive relationships with family and friends.
2. **Practice Self-Care:** Prioritize your physical and mental health.

3. Develop Emotional Awareness: Understand and manage your emotions effectively.
4. Embrace Change: View change as an opportunity for growth.
5. Set Realistic Goals: Work towards achievable goals and celebrate small successes.
6. Develop Problem-Solving Skills: Approach problems with a strategy and openness to solutions.
7. Foster Optimism: Cultivate a positive outlook and mindset.
8. Build Self-Confidence: Recognize your strengths and believe in your abilities.
9. Practice Mindfulness: Engage in mindfulness exercises to stay grounded in the present.
10. Learn from Experience: Reflect on and learn from past challenges.
11. Seek Support When Needed: Don't hesitate to ask for help from friends, family, or professionals.
12. Cultivate Gratitude: Practice gratitude regularly to focus on the positive.
13. Stay Physically Active: Exercise regularly to reduce stress and improve mood.
14. Nurture a Growth Mindset: Belief in your ability to grow and learn from experiences.
15. Embrace Challenges: View challenges as learning opportunities and strengthening resilience.
16. Practice Self-Compassion: Be kind and understanding towards yourself during tough times.
17. Maintain a Sense of Purpose: Align your actions with your values and goals.

18. Take Breaks: Give yourself time to rest and recharge.
19. Develop Healthy Coping Strategies: Identify and practice effective ways to deal with stress.
20. Stay Flexible: Be open to adjusting your approach when faced with obstacles.
21. Focus on What You Can Control: Concentrate on aspects of challenges that you can influence.
22. Volunteer or Help Others: Supporting others can enhance your sense of community and purpose.
23. Keep Learning: Continuous learning and curiosity can build resilience.
24. Avoid Catastrophizing: Steer clear of imagining the worst-case scenarios.
25. Maintain a Sense of Humour: Find humour in life, even during tough times.

Developing resilience is a continuous process and involves cultivating a balanced approach to life's challenges and stressors. Integrating these practices into your life can enhance your ability to adapt and thrive through adversity.

CHAPTER 6

Rising from the Ashes

"Sometimes when you're in a dark place, you think you've been buried, but you've actually been planted."

- Christine Caine

I was at a crossroads after the devastating storm of gossip, deception, and betrayal. I remained in the neighbourhood for five more years. My marriage, once the foundation of my life, was in shambles; its foundation was fractured and brittle. The awareness had sunk in that it was clear that the relationship I had put so much into would be irreparable. It was a terrifying prospect but also the start of a life-changing experience.

Faced with the ruins of my marriage and the scars created by false accusations, I took a firm decision to emphasise personal development and independence. This shift in focus led to self-discovery, education, career advancement, and self-improvement.

I set my sights on a brighter and more hopeful future as the flames of my past smoulder.

The power to make informed decisions, especially regarding our lives and relationships, is a profound form of self-empowerment. This section equips you with the tools and insights necessary to navigate the complex landscape of choices, enabling you to make decisions that align with your true self and vision for the future.

Recognise that at the heart of decision-making lies your autonomy—your right to choose your life and your body. Embracing this autonomy means acknowledging that you are the primary architect of your life, capable of making choices that reflect your values, needs, and aspirations. Remember, your choices are yours, and they have power.

Before making any significant decision, especially concerning your relationships or life direction, arm yourself with information. Research, seek advice from trusted sources, and consider all possible outcomes. Knowledge is power—it transforms uncertain paths into roads mapped with insight and foresight.

While facts and advice are invaluable, so too is your intuition. The internal compass guides you through the noise of external opinions and societal pressures. Dedicate time for quiet reflection, allowing your inner voice to surface. Ask yourself, "What does my gut feeling tell me?" Often, your intuition will lead you toward decisions that genuinely resonate with your core.

A simple yet effective method for decisions that leave you torn is to list the pros and cons. This exercise can help clarify the benefits and drawbacks of each option, providing a visual representation of potential outcomes. Remember, the goal is scored once you illuminate paths that best align with your goals and values.

Every decision has ripple effects, impacting your immediate and long-term future. Consider how your choice aligns with where you want to be in five, ten, or even twenty years. Asking, "Does this decision bring me closer to the person I aspire to be?" can guide you toward choices that support your growth and fulfilment.

Once you've decided, embrace it with conviction. Take the necessary steps to implement your choice, knowing that action bridges decision and outcome. Afterwards, reflect on the process—what you learned about yourself, how the decision impacted your life, and how you might approach future choices. This reflection is invaluable for honing your decision-making skills.

Not all decisions will lead to the desired outcome, and that's okay. Mistakes are not failures but growth opportunities. They teach resilience, adaptability, and the courage to make bold choices, even in uncertainty.

Empowering yourself to make informed decisions involves self-discovery, courage, and growth. It involves understanding your power of choice, gathering information, listening to your intuition, weighing your options, considering long-term impacts, taking decisive action, and learning from the outcomes. By embracing these principles, you equip yourself with the strength to navigate the complexities of life and relationships, steering your story toward a future that resonates with your most profound truths and highest aspirations.

Recognising that my marriage was maybe irreparable was a startling and heart-breaking discovery. I expected clarity and resolution after confronting Sarah about the falsehoods and false claims that had ripped through the fabric of our relationship. What happened after that conversation, however, crushed any remaining illusions I had about the future of my marriage.

When I contacted and spoke with Roland (the accused boyfriend), he was upset and expressed tremendous shock, but he was very supportive. He contacted my husband, giving him an honest description of the events, which exposed the truth behind Sarah's fabrications. It was evident that Sarah's assertions were unfounded because I was not in a relationship with this man, and he was too comfortable to be supported by me, who barely struggled to fend for myself and my children. He had a common friend with my husband who could attest to his well-established financial stability and family life in Nigeria.

As the pieces of this complicated puzzle fell into place, it became clear that the person Sarah had depicted and mentioned his name in her lies bore no similarity to the person they accused me of having an extramarital affair with. Sarah described this person as a man who fled abroad with me, looking for greener pastures and was supported by me with my husband's finances. Her lies fell apart under investigation, and the truth triumphed.

However, this realisation did not instantly heal the schism in my marriage. It simply revealed the enormity of the harm. The scars of scepticism, mistrust, and betrayal were deep, and I could no longer deny that my marriage was dangling by a thread. The troubles that had tormented us for years persisted, and the cornerstone of our relationship had been irreversibly shaken.

The arrival of the baby was a surprise, as contractions commenced prematurely, initiating a nearly 48-hour labour. Despite the prolonged process and the fact that I had not yet reached full dilation, the culmination of this journey occurred at 9:25 PM when Brandon entered the world through Caesarean section. I chose the name 'Chiebunigom,' signifying that God had given me a moment of elevation and profound gratitude. The birth of my baby boy inundated my world with boundless joy, a chapter forever etched in the pages of my life's story. I had more reasons to stay alive! Another turning point!

Fuelled by the profound love I held for my child, fortified by the challenges I had already surmounted, and driven by the aspiration for a brighter future, my pursuit of personal growth and financial autonomy surged. It was a significant choice that reflected the insight of countless people who had begun comparable paths of self-discovery and empowerment.

Eleanor Roosevelt famously remarked, "The purpose of life is to live it, to taste experience to the utmost, to reach out eagerly and without fear for a newer and richer experience." This quote spoke to me at the time. As soon as I understood that life was designed to be experienced to the fullest and that every event offered a chance for personal development and enrichment, these words became my mantra.

When Brandon reached the age of three months, I recognised the impending opportunity for him to be accepted into childcare at six months.

As we celebrated his six-month milestone, a noteworthy juncture emerged as I enrolled him in a childcare facility. This pivotal transition ushered in a transformative chapter in my life, affording me invaluable moments of respite and the capacity to partake in diverse activities and pursuits. I had to plan and set new goals!

My work and education advancement was crucial to my success and long-term goals. I realised that education was the key to opening new chances, and I vowed never to stop learning and growing as a person. I acquired the information and abilities required to create a more secure future through education.

Ultimately, I prioritised my personal development and independence to face the future with optimism and resolve. I came to see that life obstacles offered development opportunities, and by deciding not to let my past define me, I was setting a new course for a better future.

By making this decision, I overcame hardship, changed my life, and motivated others to pursue personal development and freedom.

When Brandon turned 14 months old, he still required daily care and attention.

This presented a need to readjust my plans, change my daily routines and re-evaluate my personal and professional goals while balancing the demands of single parenthood and professional ambitions.

So, I devised a precisely organised regimen to handle this delicate balancing act. Every morning, I would begin my day at 7 a.m. to drop him off at the crèche and travel on the train to college (Dublin Business School), where I dived into IT networks and infrastructure.

This daily routine was choreographed to perfection, like a well-orchestrated dance. It meant leaving my house at 7:20 a.m. and ensuring Brandon was comfortably situated at the crèche by 7:30 a.m. Following that, I would drive to the railway station, neatly park my car, and take the 7:40 train, all within a concise ten-minute timeframe. The margin for error was nearly non-existent; even a missed minute or hint of traffic could throw my perfectly planned itinerary into disarray.

His day-care routine, which ended at 6:30 p.m. every evening, was central to this balancing act. I had to ensure I was home by 6:30 p.m. every day to pick him up. This thorough planning allowed me to pursue my educational ambitions while providing my child with care and assistance.

My academic path as an IT networking and infrastructure student was engaging and time-consuming. Coursework and assignments frequently lasted well into the evening, posing another barrier in my quest for balance. During this time, I developed a strict evening schedule.

I would get up at 3 a.m. in the quiet hours when the world was deep in sleep, ensuring everyone else in the home was asleep. This gave me the priceless privacy I needed for intense study sessions. I would painstakingly go through my books, research, and projects until around 6:30 in the morning, anticipating the raucous clamour of my kids getting ready for school. I collected night shifts at odd times. Balancing employment, schooling, and being a single parent added to the intricacy of my Journey. My responsibilities as a mother remained unshakable, and pursuing education and a new career added another layer to an already overburdened plate. Late-night study sessions, juggling work commitments, and catering to my children's needs became a daily reality for me. There was no going back as I was a role model for my children.

My pre-dawn study sessions and their morning routines were separated by only two to three hours. I would take advantage of this little respite to get an hour or two of sleep. It was a credit to my determination to get a good night's sleep quickly, recharging my energy for the day ahead.

My unrelenting focus and strict regimen remained intact even as I switched from academic life to job-seeking. My approach to job applications reflected my attention to my education and parenting obligations.

When I graduated from Dublin Business School (DBS), I woke up at 3 a.m. while everyone else was still sleeping. I carefully sent my CV to numerous organisations during these calm hours to find a lucrative job. By getting an early start, I ensured that my applications reached the hiring managers before those of my competitors.

After submitting applications, I would allow myself a brief rest period, settling back to sleep after the children leave for school. However, my dedication continued during these breaks. At 9 a.m., I would rouse myself from slumber and commence a series of follow-up calls to the companies where I had submitted my CV. The goal was to confirm receipt of my application, reassuring me that my candidacy was under consideration.

I kept an organised method to keep order and follow the status of my job applications. Each application was painstakingly logged in an Excel sheet, which included vital information such as the job role, contact information for the prospective Business, and the recruiter's name. This meticulous technique enabled me to stay on top of my job search, ensuring every opportunity was noticed.

This was, without a doubt, one of the most challenging periods of my life. The rigours of single parenthood, academics, and a career created a never-ending vortex of responsibilities. Nonetheless, in this crucible, I learned essential lessons that continue to influence my Journey.

Lessons

- The period emphasised the significance of time management. My demanding daily schedule necessitated rigorous preparation and strict respect for deadlines. I learned to make the most of every minute to accomplish my responsibilities as a mom, student, and job seeker.
- This voyage emphasised the importance of resilience and adaptation. Life's unanticipated twists and turns compelled me to pivot and adjust constantly. Whether it was a schedule change for my child or negotiating the difficulties of the job market, I learned to be adaptable and tenacious in pursuing my goals.
- It increased my appreciation for the value of hard work and devotion. I survived and thrived in the face of hardship by sticking to my routines and paying close attention to detail. This phase of my life instilled in me that any problem can be surmounted with the appropriate mindset and steadfast commitment.

A fresh set of issues arose between my husband and me in the following years. Financial conflicts and my husband's growing sense of alienation drove us further apart. He had been swayed by false information regarding single moms in Ireland, believing that the government gave extravagant allowances, free houses, no school fees payment, and other supports. The reality, however, was far from these preconceptions, as single parenthood in Ireland was not a visa to free meal tickets, especially if you were working full time as I was. I battled to make ends meet and worked as a healthcare assistant on shifts, juggling the financial duties of raising my children, paying for their education, and maintaining our household while also dealing with my ambitions for self-improvement and personal development.

My husband's refusal to provide the required support and insistence on controlling our finances contributed to the stress. He demanded direct access to the landlord's account for rent payments that he wanted to pay from Nigeria (which he never did). He would buy expensive gadgets as presents for the children rather than pay for new uniforms and books because someone had informed him that education and education supplies such as books and uniforms were free in Ireland. He appeared unwilling to entrust me with any financial obligations. This lack of trust and support harmed our relationship, further convincing me that our marriage was on the brink of collapse.

The emotional divide within our marriage widened with time, presenting as a constant source of misery. Each phone call with my husband left me with a deep sense of loneliness, lowered self-esteem, and an overall decline in my well-being. He had steadfastly refused video calls since the beginning of my relocation, which had long been a source of anxiety.

Following a particularly discouraging encounter one fateful evening, I mustered the confidence to tackle the accumulating fears that had haunted me for far too long. He immediately ended the call after delivering his ideas, as was his custom. Instead of falling into the normal cycle of weeping, self-pity or sweeping it under the carpet for peace's sake, I gave him a five-day grace period to reach out and try to mend the shredding fabric of our relationship. Unfortunately, those five days passed with no attempt on his behalf to reconnect us.

In those five days, I reflected on my marital journey. The outcome of that reflection was a significant question that needed to be answered: What am I doing remaining unhappily married? At the initial stage, when I had identified that I had made a mistake, I could not reverse it because my parents had warned me that marriage was for better or worse and there would be no more room for me in the house once

I left. On several occasions when I decided to be bold and take the plunge, I remember the embarrassment I would be causing mummy and daddy. At the time, Mummy was the head of a catholic women's organisation, and the thought of her only daughter with a broken marriage sounded like a horror movie. At this stage, Dad had passed, and Mum had dementia and could hardly remember her children, let alone understand embarrassment. The entire scenario sounded like freedom, and I thought this was the right time to set things right. It's either the marriage works, or it doesn't. So, I wrote a lengthy, meaningful text message hoping to spark a discourse to reconcile and repair our marriage. I extended an olive branch even further by giving him a two-week opportunity to respond. Still, to my dismay, he stayed deafeningly silent.

At that point, the unmistakable fact dawned on me: our marriage had come to an end. In the third week, a heart-breaking phone call from home informed me of my mother's severe sickness, prompting me to return to Nigeria immediately to ensure her medical care and well-being.

After caring for my mother, I felt that treating myself with some rest, self-care, and outings was appropriate. I went to the salon, got my hair and nails done, and had a massage. Then, I contacted a few friends, and we began a night of socialising with laughter, dancing, and merriment. During our adventures, I confided in one of my buddies about my longing to see my husband. Her relentless questions prompted me to restate my objectives, and I did so.

Our investigation eventually took us to a nightclub and, to our surprise, a strip club. It was there that I ran into my estranged husband for the first time since we had the issues. It became unmistakably evident in that enlightening moment that our marriage had irreparably ended.

I could not think of a reason for this other than that he might have either fallen out of love or still saw me as the 17-year-old girl he met.

I took serious action the next week, meeting a legal professional and started divorce proceedings. There was no time to think; my fears had been confirmed, and I had to face the unavoidable fact.

In the face of these problems, I found myself at a crossroads, evaluating not just my destiny but also that of my children. The mental upheaval and harsh realities of my circumstance caused me to re-evaluate my course of action. In these moments of reflection, and against the turbulent backdrop of my marriage, I began to value personal development, independence, and the quest for a future built on my terms.

Everyone's situation is unique, and there is no one-size-fits-all solution; I can provide some general advice and suggestions in a scenario like mine. It would be best if you did not handle things alone as I did; it was too harsh to manage independently. A few suggestions are:

- Forgiveness is the starting point for any individual to achieve true healing. Forgive yourself and forgive the person or people who hurt you. Doing this relieves you of the weight of anger and allows you to move on quickly.
- Seek expert help: To cope with emotional stress, anxiety, and thoughts of self-harm, it is critical to consult with a mental health expert or therapist. They can offer advice, support, and solutions for challenging emotions.
- Assess the Relationship: Seek couples counselling or therapy to address concerns in your marriage. A professional can assist both parties in improving their communication and resolving any trust difficulties that have emerged.

- Financial Independence: Investigate financial independence possibilities if you feel financially strapped or unsupported. This may entail looking for work, upgrading job skills, or accessing social support systems to help you become self-sufficient.
- Legal Counsel: Speak with a family lawyer to learn about your rights and alternatives in your existing marriage and any prospective separation or divorce. They can get advice on child custody, financial settlements, and legal safeguards.
- Lean on support Networks: For emotional assistance, contact friends, family, or support groups. Sharing your feelings and experiences with trusted people can provide consolation and help reduce feelings of loneliness.
- Focus on Self-Care: Take care of your physical and mental health. Examples of self-care routines include exercise, meditation, and hobbies that delight you. Taking care of yourself is critical during difficult times.
- Goal setting: Consider your long-term objectives and desires for yourself and your children. Creating a clear future vision can provide motivation and a sense of purpose.
- Legal and Financial Planning: If you decide separation or divorce is the best option for you, speak with professionals who can guide you through the legal and financial parts of the process.
- Stay Informed: Be aware of community resources such as social services, shelters, and organisations that aid people in challenging situations.
- Take Your Time: Decisions made during emotional turmoil might have long-term implications. Evaluate your position,

seek competent guidance, and make informed decisions that align with your well-being and aspirations.
- Too many Advisors: Listen to your inner voice and avoid listening to advice from too many people. Your actions might not be authentic, as they may be based on external influences instead of your thoughts and feelings.

Although there were challenges along the way to independence, I remembered Nelson Mandela's adage, "It always seems impossible until it's done." This reminded me that I can overcome the most challenging obstacles with patience and determination. I clung to the hope that, like Mandela, I might overcome impossibilities and escape the limitations that had restricted me.

My odyssey required me to break free from control. It was a relief to realise that I could free myself from the limitations of my past. Like thousands, I realised I could regain control of my life.

Financial independence was a significant milestone in my pursuit of personal growth and freedom. It wasn't merely about accumulating wealth but about using that financial freedom to make a positive impact, both in my life and the lives of others. The journey towards a fulfilling future is paved with clear visions and well-defined goals.

Goal setting is not just about identifying what you want to achieve; it's about breaking these aspirations into achievable steps and creating a roadmap for success. It's about transforming dreams into actionable plans, ensuring that each step you take moves you closer to your desired life.

Here is an exercise to guide you through envisioning your future and setting inspiring and attainable goals.

Exercise

Begin by allowing yourself the space and freedom to dream. Imagine your ideal future without constraints. What does it look like? Who are you in this future? Visualisation is a powerful tool that helps clarify your desires and solidifies your commitment to pursuing them. Create a vision board or write a detailed description of your ideal future to make it more tangible.

Once you have a clear vision, it's time to define your goals. Be specific about what you want to achieve. General goals are more complex to pursue because they need more clarity. Instead of saying, "I want to be happy," define what happiness means to you. Is it a fulfilling career, a loving family, financial stability, or all the above? Specific goals are the foundation of an effective action plan.

Specific, Measurable, Achievable, Relevant, Time-bound (SMART). Transform your goals into SMART goals:

- Specific: Clearly define what you want to achieve.
- Measurable: Identify how you will measure progress and success.
- Achievable: Ensure the goal is within reach, given your current resources and constraints.
- Relevant: Make sure the goal aligns with your broader life aspirations.
- Time-bound: Set a realistic deadline for achieving the goal.

This framework gives your goals structure and makes the path to achieving them more precise and manageable.

As the saying goes, a Journey of a thousand miles starts with a step. Break your goals down into smaller, actionable steps. This makes even the most significant goals seem more attainable. Each step should be a mini goal with its timeline and success criteria. Celebrate each milestone to maintain motivation and momentum.

Part of practical goal setting is anticipating potential obstacles and planning for them. Consider what might hinder your progress and consider strategies to overcome these challenges. Being prepared doesn't mean you expect failure; you're equipped to persevere through setbacks.

Regularly review your goals and the progress you've made towards them. Life is dynamic, and your goals may need to adapt to changing circumstances or new insights. Be bold and adjust your goals if they no longer align with your vision for the future. Flexibility is a strength, not a weakness.

Setting and pursuing goals is a robust process that gives direction and purpose to your life. It's about turning your vision for the future into a concrete plan and taking deliberate steps towards making that future a reality. Remember, goal setting is not set in stone; it's a living process that evolves as you grow. With clear goals, a detailed plan, and a commitment to adapt and persevere, you are well on your way to creating the future you envision for yourself.

CHAPTER 7

The Path to Transformation

"The only way to make sense out of change is to plunge into it, move with it, and join the dance."

- Alan Watts.

We frequently meet junctures in life that require fundamental transformation, prompting us to review our choices and reinvent our identity. This Chapter delves into a critical period in my life when I was at a fork in the road. I'd already travelled far from home, seeking safety in a country, survived the storm of rumours and betrayal that threatened to consume me and was on a journey to becoming a divorcee. However, the upheaval in my personal life was far from ending.

My transformative voyage toward personal growth and self-reliance was a bold step into the unknown, fraught with difficulties and doubts for so many reasons, such as complex decision-making, steep career transitions to unfamiliar terrains, and learning new work cultures. However, it also allowed self-discovery and reinvention, urging me to embrace change zealously.

The delicate skill of combining the demands of employment, study, and single parenthood was a primary issue. This sophisticated juggling act, which could easily have overwhelmed me, became the furnace in which I developed a new professional identity. It was a complex process, but it was ultimately successful.

I experienced the transformational power of education, the importance of resilience in the face of adversity, and the tremendous influence of developing a new professional identity. It was an era of significant growth and evolution, characterised by a never-ending search for a more fantastic future. As with most successful journeys in life, I encountered difficulties and wins and learnt a lot along the way to change.

This decision to go back and study IT Network and Infrastructure was critical since it signified another fresh start in my career path, except I focused on getting a job in the IT Department of the healthcare sector; my past healthcare knowledge would be irrelevant to my newfound IT expertise. It was the point that I had to combine my past and present, harnessing the wisdom and insights I had gained from my prior job and infusing them with the knowledge in Information technology that I was gaining. It was a synthesis of knowledge and experience that fostered my metamorphosis.

Being an IT project manager in the healthcare sector in Ireland was challenging. A steep learning curve accompanied the change. I had to master the complexities of managing big IT projects, comprehending healthcare technological nuances, and adapting to a fast-paced and ever-changing sector. It required tenacity, a willingness to learn, and an unshakable dedication to personal development.

However, as I became more immersed in this new role, I experienced a wonderful sense of fulfilment. The realm of IT project management provided a blank canvas for me to create my vision of the future. It enabled me to use my leadership ability, problem-solving abilities, and acute eye for detail to drive projects to completion. It was a field that praised and rewarded those who dared to push the limits of what was possible.

Throughout this adjustment, there were different hurdles, including racial discrimination in the workplace, but my eyes were focused on my goals, and nothing would stop me. I realised that to bring about the desired change, I needed to be the catalyst for that transformation. I held on to the fact that transformation begins within, fuelled by our desires and propelled by our actions.

Looking back at the obstacles I experienced and the triumphs I attained. The significant relevance of pursuing educational goals and transitioning to a new career path as a means of personal development was well worth it. I have enjoyed the sense of success and the invaluable benefits of accepting change as a driving force for transformation. My Journey from the world of healthcare Support to the dynamic world of IT project management is a living monument to the steadfast principles of perseverance and tenacity that steered me toward a bright and promising future. Traversing the complexities of establishing a new professional identity presented several obstacles and victories that defined the essence of my path. Shifting from a career in healthcare Support to IT necessitated a thorough re-evaluation of my abilities, objectives, and self-concept.

The difficulties were numerous, frequently lying in the shadows like daunting barriers in my path. One of the most difficult challenges was retraining and learning new skills and working methods. The learning curve was severe, and doubts crept in when I faced the sharp difference between my former experience and this.

Despite these obstacles, some victories fuelled my drive to persevere. The process of creating a new professional persona demonstrated my tenacity and adaptability. Each achievement in my IT courses boosted my confidence and reinforced that transformation was possible.

Triumphant moments took many forms, from completing projects on time to passing exams. These accomplishments significantly affirm my capacity to accept change and adapt not just academic or professional achievements. They were the foundation for my developing professional identity and fostered a deep sense of pride and purpose.

Ultimately, this period was an ongoing process of growth and self-discovery. I took on obstacles head-on, finding resiliency amid hardship and resolve in the face of uncertainty. Through the struggles of switching to a new vocation, I learned the extent of my powers: my resolve, tenacity, ability to progress, the limitless possibilities for transformation, and I built confidence.

***

Single parenting is a journey marked by its unique set of challenges and rewards, a path walked with the resilience of the heart and the strength of the spirit. Accepting your situation and deliberately mapping out your way to success that aligns with your values helps to ensure a more leisurely journey. There are several intricacies of single parenthood, hurdles that must be overcome and the profound joys that can be discovered along the way. It's about recognising the duality of the experience—the tough days and triumphant days—and embracing each with grace and determination. I vividly recall occasions when financial constraints made it impossible to provide school lunches for all three of my children attending primary school. During such times, my eldest child would selflessly forgo her school lunch, allowing her two younger siblings to enjoy their meals at school, and she would wait to have a cooked lunch at home upon her return.

One of the most daunting aspects of single parenting is the constant balancing act required to manage the dual roles of provider and caregiver. The responsibility of making ends meet, coupled with the emotional and physical demands of parenting alone, can sometimes feel overwhelming. Yet, in these moments of pressure, single parents often discover their resilience, learning to navigate the complexities of life with a resourcefulness that is both necessary and empowering.

Loneliness can be a significant challenge for single parents, not just in terms of the absence of a partner but also in the solitary nature of decision-making and problem-solving. The weight of these decisions, from the mundane to the monumental, rests solely on their shoulders. However, it's also within this solitude that many single parents find a deepened sense of self-reliance and confidence in their judgment.

Steering the complexities of single motherhood, one may encounter individuals who seek to exploit the situation, positioning themselves as saviours while subtly undermining your sense of self-worth. This dynamic can be particularly challenging, as it imposes undue stress and skews the perception of your achievements and capabilities.

In the face of such challenges, the solution lies in cultivating a robust sense of self-respect and independence. Embracing your worth as an individual and a parent is paramount. Recognise that your relationship status does not define you, nor are you obligated to accept less than you deserve out of gratitude. Building a support network of friends, family, and fellow single parents can provide a solid foundation of encouragement and advice, reinforcing that you are not alone in your journey.

Moreover, setting clear boundaries with others and advocating for your needs becomes crucial in safeguarding your well-being and dignity. Asserting these boundaries is not an act of defiance but a declaration of self-respect. It's essential to surround yourself with individuals who respect these limits and understand your value beyond your single-parent status. Focusing on personal growth, self-care, and the well-being of your children forges a path of empowerment. This journey is about recognising your strength, resilience, and the unique contributions you make to your family and community. Remember, your value is intrinsic and not contingent upon the approval or assistance of others.

Societal stigma can add an external layer of difficulty, with misconceptions and judgments about single parenting still prevalent. Yet, many single parents learn to rise above these stereotypes, focusing instead on the love and bond they share with their children. In doing so, they challenge and change the narratives surrounding single parenthood, showcasing the diversity and strength of families in all forms.

Every milestone, big or small, becomes a shared victory in single parenting. These moments, from a child's first steps to their graduation, are imbued with a special significance, as both parent and child recognise the unique Journey they have navigated together. Celebrating these achievements becomes a testament to their collective resilience and love.

Single parenting is a journey of personal growth, both as an individual and as a parent. Many single parents find that their challenges lead to profound personal development, imbuing them with strength, flexibility, and a deep gratitude for the simple moments of joy. This individual evolution is not just a silver lining but a shining testament to the transformative power of single parenting.

Sailing through parenthood alone is an odyssey of love, challenge, and growth. It requires resilience, compassion, and an unyielding dedication to the well-being of one's children. Yet, within this Journey lies the opportunity for incredible joy and deep, enduring bonds. Through their unwavering commitment and love, single parents create a legacy of strength and resilience, teaching their children the value of perseverance and the depth of unconditional love.

Steering the complexities of co-parenting after a separation or divorce presents a unique set of challenges and opportunities. At the heart of this Journey is a shared commitment to the well-being and happiness of your children. Establishing healthy boundaries and effective communication with your ex-partner is crucial for fostering a stable and supportive environment for your children. This section offers practical tips for managing relationships with ex-partners, ensuring that the focus remains on nurturing and supporting your children through this transition.

Lessons

- Effective communication is the cornerstone of successful co-parenting. Establish clear and consistent communication channels with your ex-partner, choosing methods that work best for both of you, whether through text, email, or phone calls. Aim for clarity and conciseness in your exchanges, focusing on the needs and well-being of your children above all.

- Boundaries are essential for maintaining a healthy co-parenting relationship. Clearly define what is acceptable and what is not regarding communication and interactions. This includes respecting each other's privacy, adhering to agreed-upon schedules, and avoiding discussing personal matters unrelated to co-parenting. Boundaries help prevent conflicts and ensure that both parents feel respected and heard.

- A co-parenting plan can serve as a valuable roadmap, outlining how you will share responsibilities and make decisions regarding your children. This plan should cover practical aspects such as living arrangements, visitation schedules, financial obligations, and how to handle holidays and special occasions. A written agreement can minimise misunderstandings and provide a clear framework for your co-parenting relationship.

- In every decision and interaction, keep your children's needs and well-being at the forefront. This means setting aside personal grievances and focusing on what is best for your children. Encourage a positive relationship between your children and your ex-partner, speaking about them respectfully and fostering an environment where your children feel loved and secure.

- Flexibility is vital in co-parenting arrangements. Life is unpredictable, and situations may arise that require adjustments to schedules or plans. Approaching these changes with a willingness to compromise can help maintain a positive co-parenting relationship and demonstrate to your children the value of cooperation and adaptability.
- Co-parenting can be emotionally challenging. Don't hesitate to seek support from friends, family, or professionals who can offer guidance and perspective. Support groups and counselling services can also provide valuable resources and strategies for navigating the complexities of co-parenting.

Co-parenting with clear boundaries and mutual respect requires effort, patience, and a commitment to putting your children's needs first. You can create a positive co-parenting environment by establishing effective communication, setting clear boundaries, and approaching challenges with flexibility and understanding. This benefits your children's emotional and psychological well-being and fosters a sense of security and stability as they experience changes in their family dynamics.

CHAPTER 8

Blissful Beginnings

*"Do not wait until the conditions are perfect to begin.
Beginning makes the conditions perfect."*

- Alan Cohen

Looking back, I am filled with a great sense of exhilaration and expectation. This stage of my life is more than just a new chapter; it is a monument to the unwavering spirit of perseverance and growth. It is the story of self-discovery, tenacity, and the triumphant fulfilment of dreams. At this juncture, my first three children have blossomed into accomplished adults, each excelling in their respective careers and professions. Their success fills me with immense pride and signals an opportune moment for me to embark on a new chapter. With their journeys well underway, the timing feels perfectly aligned for me to venture into the uncharted territories of the business world. This transition marks not just a personal evolution but a venture filled with the promise of discovery and growth in the vast business landscape.

The completion of my MBA was a significant milestone in my educational path. Still, it was only the beginning of a more extensive search for knowledge and accomplishment. With my acquired knowledge and skills, I stepped into uncharted territories, aiming to establish a space for myself in the competitive environment of Business and management. My MBA's academic rigours and challenges had prepared me for the road ahead, and I was ready to continue a path of constant growth and development.

The need for autonomy and the desire to pursue a goal drove my decision to become an entrepreneur. It was a leap of faith, a determination to seize control of my fate and shape it to my liking. The shift from employee to business owner is defined by dangers, risks, opportunities, and the exhilaration of charting one's destiny.

The celebration of stability is central to this story. The sense of accomplishment from raising responsible children as a single parent while controlling one's future transcends monetary gains. It's a declaration of self-sufficiency, a tribute to the never-ending pursuit of success. Each element is vital in defining my story, from academic achievements to entrepreneurial endeavours and personal growth to stability. This narrative is about empowerment, daring to dream, and seizing life's opportunities. Above all, it is a story of perseverance, reminding us that every ending is only the prelude to a new and thrilling beginning.

> *"Sometimes, the smallest step in the right direction ends up being the biggest step of your life. Tiptoe if you must, but take the step."*
>
> —Naeem Callaway

First and foremost, my decision to obtain an MBA was to strengthen my business acumen. This was motivated by two key goals: the desire to start my own business and transition from the technical side of IT to the Business realm. This journey had great promise, but it also presented distinct problems.

It had a fascinating start! As soon as I entered the MBA program, I became aware I was the only person of colour among my peers. I was still determining whether I had made the appropriate choice because I had previously experienced racial bigotry and discrimination. I was pleasantly pleased, nevertheless, by how enthusiastically and warmly my classmates welcomed me. There were 25 more experts in respective fields, all world-class. This multicultural community embraced me and created an atmosphere where I felt respected and valued. We got along well, and this camaraderie led to some strong friendships.

The MBA program proved to be a life-changing experience for me. At the time, I was still dealing with self-esteem and confidence issues arising from earlier experiences that had left their imprint. I was figuring out how to approach individuals or properly communicate my ideas. I set out on my educational adventure, hoping to learn and improve.

The program divided us into groups of five. Our lecturers once urged us to share our life experiences and personal histories with other group members if we felt comfortable doing so. I was initially hesitant to discuss my past. However, I recognised that if I wanted to evolve and transform genuinely, I needed to let go of the baggage of my past. Without hesitation, I decided to share my entire life journey, from my childhood to my marriage, my voyage from Nigeria, and my life raising my children to that time. I didn't hold anything back.

Surprisingly, this act of vulnerability and openness transformed my outlook on life. It felt liberating. I discovered that after pouring out my soul to my group, there was nothing left to conceal or be ashamed of, regardless of whether the experiences were sound, awful, or downright ugly. That realisation changed my perspective and allowed me to approach life with fresh freedom.

This transformative experience had a tremendous impact on my two-year college journey, notably during my MBA. During the program's second year, I had the opportunity to fly to New York for a Leadership course with my team. Because of the solid foundation of trust and camaraderie we had established, integrating with my peers during this trip was effortless. Our partnership was built on the relationships developed during our open chats and shared experiences.

In retrospect, my MBA program was beneficial. It provided me with helpful business knowledge, changed my thinking, and increased my confidence. The lessons I acquired in and out of the classroom shaped my outlook on life and my everlasting confidence in the power of vulnerability, openness, and genuine human connections.

A mixture of enthusiasm and apprehension frequently marks the Journey into entrepreneurship; mine was no exception. The choice to go into Business and start my own company signified a giant step towards financial independence and pursuing my aspirations. It was a voyage motivated by a desire to break free from the confines of traditional employment and forge my path.

The groundwork for this entrepreneurial venture was established while pursuing my MBA. This transformative educational experience provided me with the information, skills, and confidence required to negotiate the complex world of Business. My MBA completion constituted a defining moment when theory met practice, and my ambitions began to take shape.

I leapt forward and formally began my business, which started to shape up in eight months. While it is still in its early phases at this writing, its development and success are encouraging. Every step, from establishing the company to managing its day-to-day operations, has been a learning experience. It demonstrates the strength of perseverance and the desire to make dreams a reality.

Entrepreneurship is complex, and I have encountered my fair share. The uncertainty, financial hazards, and the weight of responsibility can all be intimidating. However, the sense of independence, the chance to chart my path, and the possibility of financial benefits make this journey extremely satisfying.

As I continue to create and nurture my company, I am reminded that entrepreneurship is more than simply making money; it is about creating something meaningful, offering value to clients, and giving back to the community. It's about taking charge of my future and pursuing a vision with tenacity.

Starting a business has been a voyage of self-discovery, resilience, and pursuing a goal. It is a journey that is still unfolding, filled with challenges and victories, but ultimately guided by the notion that everything is possible with hard work, dedication, and the willingness to embrace the unknown.

"The biggest adventure you can take is to live the life of your dreams."

- Oprah Winfrey.

I am overwhelmed with profound introspection and thankfulness. From blister to bliss, my Journey has been revolutionary and altered my life and worldview.

A journey distinguished by self-discovery, resilience, and the steadfast quest for happiness.

The path from blister to bliss is challenging and bumpy. It has been sprinkled with difficulties that have put my mettle to the test, setbacks that have pushed me to my limits, and moments of doubt that have tried to obscure the route forward. But because of these difficulties, I have matured, learnt priceless lessons, and emerged more robust and empowered.

After going through the tumultuous waters of personal transformation, entering new relationships can feel like stepping into uncharted territory. The latter part of this Chapter is dedicated to guiding you as you open your heart to new connections confidently and clearly. It's about acknowledging your past experiences as valuable lessons that have prepared you for this moment, allowing you to approach new relationships from a place of strength and self-awareness.

This chapter is a thoughtful interlude, a pause to consider the stepping stones that have led me here. It's a chance to share the insights I've received, the wisdom I've gained from experience, and the joy of living with an open heart.

I've been a student of life throughout this voyage, absorbing its lessons and applying them to my progress. The lessons I've learned cover the gamut of human experience: overcoming adversity, the strength of steadfast faith, the importance of crafting one's path, and the transformational power of personal growth.

My personal development has been nothing short of a rebirth, a shedding of old skin to allow for the emergence of a stronger, more confident version of myself. I've learned the breadth of my skills, knowing I have the fortitude to weather any storm and the tenacity to recover from life's most abrasive blows.

This journey has been built on empowerment. True empowerment, I've realised, comes from inside, from a steadfast trust in one's skills and the determination to craft a path that coincides with one's hopes and objectives. It is the knowledge that one can shape one's destiny.

As I ponder the odyssey that has led me from blister to bliss, I am filled with hope and optimism for the future. The future is an open book, its pages awaiting the stories of my continuous development, fulfilment, and contributions to the world. I welcome the upcoming difficulties and opportunities, knowing that each contains the opportunity for more profound development and delight.

Life is frequently compared to a journey, an odyssey filled with ups and downs and moments of tremendous success. As I embark on a contemplative journey, retracing my odyssey from the scalding crucible of adversity to the uncharted territories of bliss and self-discovery, I am not only compelled but deeply motivated to share the profound lessons and experiences that have shaped this transformative path. This Journey, distinguished by unflinching tenacity, unshakeable faith that has lighted the darkest places, and an insatiable quest for personal empowerment, has not only illuminated but also stitched the intricate tapestry of life itself.

Lessons

- This convoluted Journey has taught me that personal growth does not follow a straight line. It meanders, spirals, and dances across highs and lows, with each phase uniquely contributing to my progress and self-improvement.
- I've realised that problems, those seemingly insurmountable impediments, are doors to opportunity. They put us to the test, pushed us to find strengths we didn't know we had, and ultimately served as catalysts for growth and transformation.
- Throughout this adventure, independence and stability have emerged as beacons of emancipation. Independence has been incredibly liberating. Accumulating wealth is essential but using one's position to make a difference in the lives of others, the sense of security, contentment, self-sufficiency and hard work that comes with it is key.
- I've realised the power of big goals and dreams.
- This Journey has demonstrated the significant influence of making continuous, albeit tiny, efforts toward our goals. Rather than waiting for seismic upheavals or massive transformations, the consistent accumulation of these small activities leads to significant development and transformation.
- I've understood that our thoughts heavily influence our experiences. Maintaining a positive attitude in the face of hardship is critical. Choosing not to be defined or diminished by previous problems and instead focusing on the limitless possibilities of the future is a powerful act of empowerment.

While I reflect on these life-changing experiences, I am vividly aware that my odyssey is far from over. Life continues, providing new chapters full of obstacles, lessons, and the promise of blissful moments. This voyage demonstrates that life is an ever-changing tale, waiting for us to write our own stories, take opportunities, and shape our destinies.

Here are some more reflections on the Journey from blister to bliss that may be helpful:

Reflections

i. Resilience—The Forging Force: Throughout this transforming journey, I've realised that resilience is more than just weathering life's storms; it's a dynamic force that can change misfortune into opportunity. With each new problem, I realised that resilience could be used to turn obstacles into stepping stones, moving me ahead on the path to personal progress and fulfilment.

ii. Faith as a Driving Force: Faith emerged as my constant companion amid adversity and uncertainty. This faith, not just in the external conditions but also, more crucially, in Jehovah, my abilities and the possibility of a better future, propelled my advancement. Even when the road ahead seemed uncertain, this unwavering faith in God kept me going.

iii. Origin of Empowerment: I've learned that true empowerment does not emerge from outside sources or situations; it blooms from inside. The foundation of empowerment is the notion that I have control of my life. It's the realisation that I control my destiny (Of course, not without God), allowing me to make intentional decisions that affect the trajectory of my life. This Journey has demonstrated the enormous shift that occurs when one accepts the inherent power of self-determination.

iv. Personal Growth Is Not a Linear Journey: I've realised that personal growth is not a straight line. Instead, it looks like a twisting, uncertain path with peaks and dips. While there have been exhilarating highs and trying lows, I've discovered that each stage adds immensely to my continued evolution and self-improvement, regardless of its nature. This understanding has enabled me to accept the complete range of experiences as vital lessons on my Journey to becoming the best version of myself.

v. Obstacles as transformational Catalysts: Throughout this Journey, I've experienced the fundamental fact that obstacles are not insurmountable roadblocks but hopeful chances for growth and transformation. Every adversity was a catalyst, propelling me with fresh resilience and wisdom. As I weathered life's ups and downs, I gradually adjusted my perspective, learning to see adversities as essential companions on the path to personal progress rather than opponents.

vi. The Power of Incremental Progress: One of the most eye-opening discoveries on this path has been the realisation that substantial changes can result from the cumulative influence of little, regular steps. Rather than waiting for massive transformations to occur, I learned that taking thoughtful, gradual steps toward my goals is significantly more beneficial. When knitted together over time, these seemingly insignificant acts have prepared the way for significant growth, demonstrating that consistent attention to small steps may lead to deep and long-lasting improvements in one's life.

vii. The Empowering Force of Purpose: My Journey highlighted a vital reality about the importance of purpose in life. I've grown to appreciate the importance of having a purpose that reaches beyond oneself, emphasising the enormous impact we can have on the lives of others. It serves as a reminder that true fulfilment is found not only in personal accomplishment but also in the ability to boost and positively contribute to the well-being of others around us. This realisation has strengthened my resolve to align my Journey with a purpose that aligns with my values and the greater good.

viii. The Transformative Influence of Mindset: Throughout my transformative Journey, I've discovered that mindset plays a critical part in moulding our experiences. The capacity to retain a positive outlook amid hardship is a crucial skill. It represents an intentional decision not to be constrained or defined by past struggles but rather to focus unwaveringly on the limitless possibilities of the future. This adjustment in viewpoint allows us to face hurdles with tenacity and commitment, making seemingly insurmountable obstacles on our way appear conquerable. It emphasises the tremendous power of a positive mindset in propelling our lives to greater heights.

ix. The Unending Odyssey: Reflecting on this incredible Journey is a poignant reminder that life is a never-ending adventure. Each Chapter brings new obstacles, teaches essential lessons, and reveals pockets of pure happiness. It's a never-ending odyssey, a story constantly changing and waiting to be written with the ink of experiences, emotions, and dreams.

These profound observations are a living testament to the profound progress, steadfast resilience, and enduring empowerment that have characterised my Journey from the arid lands of hell to the ecstatic realms of ecstasy. They embody the metamorphosis that occurs when one faces adversity with persistence, learns from every fall, and emerges with a better understanding of oneself and the world. Each reflection reflects the unbreakable spirit propelling me on this remarkable Journey, driving me towards a future adorned with hope, positivity, and limitless promise.

***

Before embarking on new relationships, it's crucial to have a deep understanding of your worth. This self-awareness acts as a compass, guiding your interactions and helping you establish respectful connections, nurture them, and align with your values. Recognise that you deserve love and respect, and carry this knowledge into every new relationship you forge.

One of the most empowering aspects of entering new relationships is the ability to set clear boundaries. Boundaries are not barriers but expressions of what you need to feel respected and valued in a relationship. Be open and honest about your boundaries from the outset and respect the boundaries of others in return. This mutual respect creates a solid foundation for any relationship.

Your intuition is a powerful tool for navigating new relationships. It can offer guidance when something feels right or raise alarms when something feels amiss. Learn to trust this inner voice and let it inform your decisions. If you feel uneasy or overly anxious about a new relationship, step back and explore these feelings further. Your intuition often knows what your conscious mind is yet to realise.

Vulnerability is often seen as a weakness but is a profound strength in forming deep and meaningful relationships. Allow yourself to be open about your feelings, fears, and hopes. While this may feel daunting, it invites genuine connection and understanding. Remember, vulnerability is a two-way street; it requires a willingness to share and to listen, creating a space where trust can flourish.

Clear, honest communication is the bedrock of any strong relationship. Approach new relationships with a commitment to open dialogue, expressing your thoughts and feelings with respect and kindness. Encourage your potential partner to do the same. This level of communication builds trust and ensures that both parties feel heard and valued.

While new relationships can be exhilarating, it's crucial to be careful, maintain your independence and continue nurturing your personal growth. A healthy relationship is one in which individuals can grow together without losing their sense of self. Pursue your interests and passions and support your partner in doing the same. This balance of togetherness and independence is critical to a fulfilling relationship.

Entering new relationships with confidence and clarity is a journey of balance—balancing openness with boundaries, vulnerability with strength, and togetherness with independence. Armed with the lessons of your past and a clear sense of your worth, you can forge meaningful, enriching connections reflective of the person you have become. Remember, every new relationship is an opportunity to learn, grow, and expand the horizons of your heart. Embrace these opportunities with openness, and let the Journey unfold.

As I stand at the threshold of concluding my odyssey, I am vividly aware that this is not the end but the start of a new phase—a continuation of the Journey that has carried me from blister to bliss. In this final Chapter, I provide a message of inspiration and encouragement rather than a farewell, proving that every ending is a forerunner to a new beginning. The closing words of this narrative mark the end of one Chapter and the start of another, for life, like an eternal novel, keeps unfolding with new adventures and chances waiting to be welcomed. I hope the lessons and experiences recounted on these pages may serve as a guiding light for those embarking on their voyage, illuminating the way to resilience, empowerment, and the limitless possibilities that lay beyond the horizon. So, as we reach "The End" in this Chapter, remember that it represents the beginning of a new, adventurous journey packed with unwritten chapters and undiscovered places, not its conclusion.

My life has continued to evolve and unfold in ways I could never have anticipated during the most challenging moments of my Journey since the events detailed in this book. I've ventured into new experiences, faced new obstacles, and enjoyed incredible victories. Throughout it all, I've realised the enormous value of Authenticity in constructing a successful and meaningful life.

Authenticity is more than just a phrase; it's a guiding philosophy I live by daily. It's about being true to myself, accepting my flaws and strengths, and living by my values and beliefs.

Furthermore, I've discovered that sincerity is critical to good leadership. By leading authentically, I've inspired and motivated my team, resulting in a great and productive work atmosphere. I've learned that Authenticity in leadership means establishing a vision and being upfront about my struggles and shortcomings, which humanises me and develops a culture of transparency and accountability.

Authenticity has also played an essential part in my relationships. Being genuine to myself has allowed me to connect with others on a deeper level. It's about being vulnerable, expressing feelings, and communicating openly and honestly. This has resulted in deeper bonds with my family and friends, providing a sense of belonging and support.

In the future, my dedication to Authenticity will not waver. I wish to continue embracing my authentic self personally and professionally. This includes remaining true to my principles, expressing my truth, and remaining open to growth and self-improvement. Authenticity is a journey, not a destination, and I'm excited to see where it takes me.

As I proceed, I'm reminded of a Brené Brown quote: "Authenticity is a collection of choices that we have to make every day." These words speak to me deeply. I strive to make such decisions every day, embracing Authenticity as a guiding light on my ongoing Journey, which is why one of the books of the Blister to Bliss series is focused on Embracing Authenticity.

A message of inspiration and encouragement

As I stand on the verge of a new chapter in my life, one thing is clear: My odyssey from blister to bliss has not only transformed my past but also enlightened my future. Looking ahead, I am accompanied by unshakeable hope and positivity.

The Journey that led me here has been one of the winding twists and unexpected turns paved by tenacity and resolve. I've emerged more robust and with a fresh purpose from its hardships and tribulations. This Journey has taught me that life is an ever-changing adventure, a never-ending novel waiting to be told.

Hope burns within me like a steady flame. It is the conviction that tomorrow will bring new starts, new opportunities, and unknown territory to explore. Hope feeds the path, providing hope even in the darkest times. The whisper inspires me to dream, aspire, and reach the heavens.

Positivity, too, is a guiding star in my life's constellation. It is the lens through which I see the world, a perspective that gives even the most difficult situations a silver lining. Positivity reminds me that behind every setback is a hidden opportunity, and the seeds of growth are behind every obstacle. It is my thoughts that allow me to weather storms.

Looking ahead, I am grateful for the lessons learned along the Journey. Each difficulty has been a teacher, each obstacle a stepping stone, and each success a tribute to the human spirit's endurance. The past has formed me but does not define me; it is the foundation for a brighter future.

The road ahead may be fraught with uncertainty and difficulty, but it is one I eagerly anticipate. It's a painting begging to be painted with the colours of experience, an embroidery begging to be woven with the threads of development.

I want to express my sincere gratitude to everyone who has travelled with me through the pages of this book for sharing my experiences, hardships, and victories. It has been a privilege to have you by my side as I sailed through the frequently choppy waters of life, and I hope that the tale of my adventure has inspired and uplifted you.

As we all know, life is not a straight and level road but a complex web of meandering paths, unforeseen detours, and sporadic barriers. However, in these turns and twists, we find our best chances for development, resiliency, and empowerment.

Keep in mind that, like mine, your Journey is continuing. It's a never-ending journey full of insightful lessons, opportunities for personal development, and blissful moments. Your voyage is still unfinished; it is an unwritten story.

I want to leave you with these words from Ralph Waldo Emerson as I conclude this Chapter of my life's narrative: "What lies behind us and what lies before us are tiny matters compared to what lies within us." May you discover the courage, fortitude, and sincerity to steer your route with optimism, hope, and steadfast resolve.

THE END

Afterword

As we close the chapter "My Odyssey: Reframing Regrets, Moving from Guilt to Growth," it's crucial to recognise that every ending heralds the beginning of a new journey. This book's conclusion is not the end but a gateway to new opportunities. Therefore, I warmly invite you to extend this journey with me beyond the confines of this book. Let us take this step forward together into the future that awaits.

Please subscribe to our newsletter for further insights, strategies, and stories that light the path ahead. You will also receive a free eBook on practical tips for enhancing self-esteem and fostering relationships. By subscribing, you become an integral part of a thriving community dedicated to growth, resilience, and transformative change.

I encourage you to engage with our vibrant social media community by following @blistertobliss on Instagram and Facebook. Here, we continue to share inspiration, practical advice, and the collective wisdom of those who have traversed similar paths. Together, we shall delve into the challenges and changes, supporting each other towards a life marked by purpose, joy, and limitless possibilities.

Thank you for joining me on this odyssey. May your journey be filled with moments of bliss, continuous growth, and unwavering hope.

With heartfelt gratitude and eternal optimism for your journey ahead.

Angela

About the Author

Angela Afieghe, a dynamic leader from Nigeria, is the CEO of Nuvie Consulting and the visionary founder of EventBooth. She holds an MBA from the University of Galway and degrees in Electronics, Computer Engineering, with ongoing studies in Event Management at the time of publication. Certified as a Project Management Professional and Scrum Master, Angela's career spans Retail, IT, Healthcare, Telecommunications, and Banking sectors.

She has honed her skills through programs at prestigious institutions like Harvard Business School and Gabrielli School of Business and is a member of esteemed organizations like the Project Management Institute and Toastmasters International. Her book series 'Blister to Bliss' delves into her experiences navigating single parenthood while excelling in education and professional growth.

Angela, a seasoned IT expert at Nuvie Consulting, specialises in developing customised IT solutions that optimise business operations. As an adept event manager, she skillfully coordinates bespoke events from inception to completion. Her latest innovation, Eventbooth, emerges as a comprehensive, one-stop event management solution, greatly enhancing the capabilities of event professionals.

Please Review

Dear reader,

If you enjoyed this book, I would really appreciate if you could leave a review on Amazon or Goodreads. Your opinion counts, and it influences buyer decisions on whether to purchase the book or not. Reviews can also open doors to new and bigger audiences for the author and helps get this book into the hands of those who most need to hear its message. Thank you.

Angela

www.ingramcontent.com/pod-product-compliance
Lightning Source LLC
Chambersburg PA
CBHW041308110526
44590CB00028B/4287